Aging without Apology

Aging without Apology
Living the Senior Years with Integrity and Faith

Robert E. Seymour

Judson Press ® Valley Forge

Aging without Apology: Living the Senior Years with Integrity and Faith
© 1995
Judson Press, Valley Forge, PA 19482-0851

Unless otherwise indicated, Scripture quotations in this volume are from *The Holy Bible*, King James Version. (KJV) Other quotations are from the *Good News Bible*, the Bible in Today's English Version. Copyright © American Bible Society, 1976. Used by permission. (GNB); The New King James Version. Copyright © 1972, 1984 by Thomas Nelson Inc. (NKJV); HOLY BIBLE: *New International Version*, copyright © 1973, 1978, 1984. Used by permission of Zondervan Bible Publishers. (NIV); the New Revised Standard Version of the Bible, copyright 1989 by the Division of Christian Education of the National Council of the Churches of Christ in the USA. Used by permission. All rights reserved. (NRSV); *The New Testament: An American Translation* by Edgar J. Goodspeed, Copyright © 1923, 1948 by the University of Chicago (Goodspeed).
"With Age Wisdom," in COLLECTED POEMS 1917—1982 by Archibald MacLeish. Copyright © 1985 by The Estate of Archibald MacLeish. Reprinted by permission of Houghton Mifflin Co. All rights reserved.
Dylan Thomas: Poems of Dylan Thomas. Copyright 1952 by Dylan Thomas. Reprinted by permission of New Directions Publishing Corp.

Library of Congress Cataloging-in-Publication Data
Seymour, Robert E. (Robert Edward), 1925-
    Aging without apology: living the senior years with integrity & faith/ by Robert E. Seymour.
    p. cm.
    ISBN 0-8170-1222-2
    1. Aging—Religious aspects—Christianity. 2. Christian life-Baptist authors.
I. Title.
    BV4580.S48 1995
    248.8'5—dc20   94-39632

Printed in the U.S.A.

95 96 97 98 99 00 01 02   8 7 6 5 4 3 2

Dedicated to

Pearl Francis Seymour, My Companion in Aging
and to
The Friends of the Chapel Hill Senior Center

Contents

Foreword

By Charles Kuralt

I met a man once who always thought there ought to be a straight highway from Duluth to Fargo. The state of Minnesota wouldn't build it, so Gordon Bushnell decided he was just going to have to build it himself. He was a wonderful, bright, and determined man. He worked on his road winter and summer for twenty-five years with nothing but a number two shovel and a wheelbarrow and an ancient John Deere tractor. When I met him, he had finished about eleven miles through the farm fields and tamarack swamps. He had about 180 miles to go. And he was seventy-eight years old at the time. By then, it wasn't the road that he cared about so much. It was building the road. What Mr. Bushnell was doing, in Robert Seymour's splendid title phrase, was growing old without apology.

Then there was Bill Bodisch. He was an Iowa farmer. When he reached his sixties, he realized he always had hated farming. So he built a great steel yacht in his barnyard, bending the steel himself, welding the joints and forging the brass propeller himself. He installed big red and green ashtrays as lenses for the running lights. Then, though he'd never even been in a rowboat before, he sold the farm, launched his boat, and sailed away down the Mississippi with his wife, Mamie, outward bound to see the world. He sent me a postcard from the Bahamas. Bill Bodisch wasn't young any more, but he didn't have any more corn to harvest or cattle to feed any more, either. He was carefree at last, a happy man. No apologies.

Here's another example closer to home. My own father worked hard as a social work administrator. He put his heart into it—days, nights, and weekends. He was so innovative and effective that they eventually named a teaching chair for him in the University of North Carolina School of Social Work at Chapel Hill and put his name on the Social Services building in Charlotte. When he retired at sixty-five after a long career in the public arena, I was terribly worried that he'd be unsettled by a life of peace and quiet. But I underestimated my father's inner resources. He found deep satisfaction in simple things: planting fruit trees in the yard of the retirement house on the North Carolina Outer Banks, regularly supplying the folks at the bank and the town hall with flowers from his garden, delivering the neighbors fresh crabmeat from his crab pots, carving toys for the children who delighted in their acquaintance with him. I think the twenty years of my father's retirement were the richest years of his life. All pleasure. No apologies.

Now I am newly retired myself and pondering the same questions about the future that Gordon Bushnell, Bill Bodisch, and my father must have pondered. Each of them found ways to grow old creatively, even triumphantly. Now that it is my turn to try the same, I am glad to have Robert Seymour's thoughtful and thorough book as a primer. His pertinent anecdotes and sensitive ruminations on the subject of aging speak to me. If I understand what he is saying, it is this: you're never really old until your regrets about the past begin to outnumber your dreams for the future.

Introduction

I am an adult in the over-sixty-five category, and I feel like a pioneer exploring uncharted territory. Although I have arrived at a stage in my life that may legitimately be labeled "old," I do not feel as I had anticipated people of my age group should feel. It is a time of considerable activity, vital interest in the world around me, and of anticipating challenges yet to be undertaken.

Professionally I have completed a forty-year career as a pastor. Thirty of those years were spent with the same congregation, so I have seen many people move from their forties into their sixties and from their fifties into their seventies. I have helped them handle midlife crises and listened to their anxieties as they approached their latter years. Some suffered a late-life crisis in anticipation of growing old.

I have enjoyed close associations with older people all of my adult life. One of the expectations of every clergyman is that he or she keep in close touch with the senior members of the congregation. There is always a long list of "shut-ins," older people confined to home due to frailty or infirmity, who appreciate frequent visits to offset loneliness. Active and healthy seniors also welcome the pastor's friendship and personal attention. Now that I have become an older adult myself, I find that my vocational exposure to elderly people is serving me well as I relate to my peers. I must admit, however, the necessity of having to reassess some of the assumptions I once had about older people when I was younger. For example, I never realized that there could be such continuity of life as one enters old age. I had anticipated more radical change.

The particular event that prompted this book was my response to a telephone call from the geriatric faculty of the University of North Carolina Medical School. I was apprised of a forthcoming southeast regional conference of health professionals who work with elderly people. The purpose of the conference was to make available to attendees the most current information about the aging process. Apparently, in the course of planning the event, someone had noted the absence of an important aspect of aging, and I was being asked to speak on the topic that might otherwise have been omitted. The missing topic was spirituality. I accepted the assignment and thus began a more careful exploration of this dimension of human life as it affects one's final years.

Other current associations converged to accentuate my interest in aging. Coinciding with my retirement five years ago, I was asked to accept an appointment to the advisory board of the Orange County Department on Aging. This seemed a logical place to invest some time and energy as I entered life's last years, working with those whom I had respected and loved throughout my professional career. One such involvement led to another. Now I serve on the boards of the Carol Woods Retirement Community, a continuing-care facility on the edge of Chapel Hill, and the Chapel Hill Home Health Agency, a large not-for-profit health-care delivery group whose clients are mainly seniors.

My major involvement with issues affecting the aging population began when I was asked to chair a task force appointed by the Orange County commissioners to assess the possible need for a new senior center in our community. Chapel Hill has experienced rapid growth and is widely recognized as one of the best places in the nation for people to retire, thus attracting large numbers of older adults. The need for a new center was easily documented and finally led to the founding of a commodious facility that is a source of pride for the entire town, and I served as the first president of The Friends of the Chapel Hill Senior Center, the nonprofit support arm of the center's operation.

Another area of my involvement is health care for seniors. At Carol Woods I am a member of the Ethics Committee, which wrestles with decisions relative to the care of terminally ill elderly people. I have also served on a task force committed to encouraging our local hospital to become more geriatric friendly. We sought ways to make it easier for older people to access physicians and to find their way through the bureaucracy. One further aim was to require special training for geriatric caregivers so that they would be more sensitive to the particular needs of patients in this age group.

There is a higher percentage of older Americans now than ever before in the history of our nation. Medical science has added years to our lives, extending them far beyond the life expectancy of previous generations. We are witnessing what many call "the graying of America." When I was young it was exceptional for people to live beyond sixty-five, but today, according to Dr. Mark Williams of the University of North Carolina Medical School, over 80 percent will live past that age. Indeed, the fastest-growing group in the country comprises men and women who are over eighty-five! Senior adults outnumber teenagers, and when the baby boomers enter retirement, the elderly population will reach a record high of 20 percent.

This rapidly growing number of senior citizens is already causing many repercussions in our society. Not only are we more visible, we also have a greater voice in every part of our corporate life. We are better educated than the generation who preceded us, and we generally have more money. Social Security provides for everyone's basic needs, and many old people enjoy an affluent lifestyle, but a sizable minority still live below the poverty level.

This unprecedented population shift in the makeup of our nation has alerted the academic world to the importance of gerontological studies, especially the new phenomena of the many very old people. Findings from current research are counter to some of the traditional understandings of the aging process, which are now being called into question. One such volley was fired recently by Betty Friedan in her new book, *Fountain of Age*, in which she advocates a new approach to aging that would significantly alter the prevailing perceptions of older people in our society in much the same way that her earlier book, *The Feminine Mystique*, changed the image of women in American culture. Friedan protests the idea that old age is a disease to be cured and insists that it is best understood as a new stage of life with indeterminate potential for continuing growth.

I share the conviction that continuing growth is a reasonable and desirable goal for all who are aging, especially growth in spirituality. I write this book not as a professional gerontologist nor as a sociologist, but simply as an aging clergyman who is intentionally introspective about what is happening to me as I continue to add candles to my birthday cakes. Much that follows represents my own opinions only, but I believe many older adults will identify with my understanding and feel they have been understood.

Everyone wants to live a long time, but no one wants to grow old. The prevalence of this sentiment reveals widespread negative impressions about the latter years of life. In contrast to this, I contend that a strong case can be made for Robert Browning's astonishing claim:

> *Grow old along with me!*
> *The best is yet to be,*
> *The last of life, for which the first was made . . .*[1]

I further contend that the likelihood of this occurring is enhanced by welcoming one's last years as an opportunity for a spiritual pilgrimage. Significantly, the next line of Browning's poem reads, "Our times are in His hand . . ." With this thought in mind, I submit what follows to all who are entering the expanding frontier of aging and who believe that spiritual direction will put them on the best-marked trail to complete life's long journey.

Chapter 1

Coming to Terms with Your Self-Image

As we grow older we welcome the ritual-like words of friends we haven't seen for a while, usually spoken in the first minutes of conversation: "You haven't changed!" We accept their comment as a compliment, for we like to think of ourselves as looking younger than we are. Their judgment confirms what we want to believe. Yet we realize that generally the observation is stretching the truth, for we have changed.

If you ponder the implications of being told you haven't changed, you might not consider it too flattering. Would we really like to keep our life on hold? I hope I have done some growing and maturing in the course of the years. But obviously the person speaking has only our physical appearance in mind, and we all appreciate being told that there is little evidence of our aging.

There are three stages of life: childhood, youth, and "My, but you're looking well!" I heard this exclamation repeatedly at the recent forty-fifth reunion of my seminary class. Several close friends had changed so much that I failed to recognize them. (But of course I softened the shock of seeing my peers by my biased judgment that I looked much younger than they did.)

Our culture is engaged in a pervasive conspiracy to keep us in a state of denial about growing old. Recently I went into a large news store to peruse the hundreds of magazines on display and to see how many, if any, were aimed at people over sixty-five. With so many people of advanced age in American society, I thought I would find new periodicals that targeted this segment of the reading public. Not so. When I asked the manager for assistance, the only magazine he could

1

offer was *Modern Maturity*, the publication of the American Association of Retired Persons (AARP)! Clearly, the publishing industry understands that Americans do not want to admit they are old. Subsequently, I have noted several church magazines for senior adults, all published by a denominational press for older members or circulated by retirement boards for religious professionals only.

Advertisers also understand how sensitive most people are about age, and they exploit it daily. They bombard us with endless television commercials that promise to make old people appear younger than they are. For example, Ponds pushes the "Age-Defying Complex" to wipe away those tell-tale wrinkles. There is a hair-coloring ad promoting "Just for Men" that features a wife exclaiming as she admires her husband, "It's like he took off ten years!" Delta Airlines promotes its senior-discount coupons with the slogan "You're Only Young Twice." If everyone responded to such pandering the way I do, profits would plummet. I am offended by the implication that my age is not acceptable and that I need to alter my appearance to deceive people about how old I really am. We should be able to feel good about ourselves no matter how many birthdays are behind us, but the ads imply that unless we conceal our age we will be judged unpresentable.

Advertising that promises to stop the aging clock is directed more toward women than men. It pictures the ideal woman as one who looks remarkably young no matter what her age. Not until recently, since the number of senior adults has increased so rapidly, has there been a significant featuring of older women as fashion models, but even they seldom present images that real older women can meet. (Some older women admit to a strange paradox: the freedom they feel once they reach an age beyond which it is futile to yield to the temptations of cosmetic camouflage.)

Twice a year our senior center sponsors a fashion show in cooperation with a large department store as a fund-raising event. The staff members of the store select outfits for the models we choose. We deliberately seek people at every stage of the aging process to participate, but sometimes we are appalled by the loud and faddish kinds of apparel they ask people to wear. The models confess to feeling that they are literally in costumes because they would seldom choose for themselves most of the outfits featured in the show.

I hope the assumption that old people are obsessed with a need to perpetuate their youth will be tempered as our numbers grow. Why can't we understand that attempts to turn back the clock are against our own best interest? The Chinese make this point in a story of a man born old with white hair and a beard. As the years went by, gradually his hair turned black, his eyes began to laugh, and his mind cleared of all worries and anxieties. When he finally neared death, his cheeks became those of a little child and were covered with an infant fuzz. Is this what we want? Surely it makes much more sense to look forward to the future and to believe our final years can be numbered among the best years of our lives. We are not likely to find genuine happiness in vain attempts to reverse the aging process, but rather in an honest acceptance of our full measure of years. Like children who love to hold up another finger on their birthdays to boast that they are another year older, so should we take pride in every additional year that passes.

But we are seldom willing to put ourselves in the "old" category. We reserve that label for anyone who is ten years older than we are! Even senior-adult church groups resist, as indicated by the young-sounding names they choose for themselves. In my own congregation the members of the senior fellowship refer to themselves as "Prime Timers," and senior adults in a neighboring church call themselves "Keen-Agers."

The number of people who are submitting to cosmetic surgery has risen to more than two million annually, making this practice seem acceptable as a way to get rid of signs of aging. Cosmetic surgery has become one of the most financially lucrative practices of the medical profession, more than a billion-dollar industry. Many candidates for these surgical procedures are older adults who balk when anyone refers to them as senior citizens, such as the woman who proudly showed me a picture of her first grandchild and then quickly said, "But don't you dare ever call me a grandmother!"

Although our new senior center reaches a broad cross

section of older people from nearly every economic and ethnic group in town, we have an outreach program to make sure all sixty-plus residents in the area know what is available for them there. But we must be careful in the way we get the word out because some people act as if they have been insulted when we suggest they are old enough to participate. "I don't want to associate with all those old people!" is a familiar refrain. My stock reply is, "It's all relative; you can always find someone at the center who is older than you are." I would prefer to say, "It's no disgrace to be seventy; relax, stop the pretense, and enjoy being the age you are."

I must confess, however, that I can identify with the temptation to want to appear younger than I am, for an odd reality of the aging process is the discrepancy between the way one feels inside and the way one looks outside. Most young people think that when a person looks old, he or she *feels* old. At some point in the aging process, this may be true for the very old, but most senior adults don't feel significantly different than they ever did. One woman put it this way:

> *Whenever I look in the mirror I sometimes feel that I am not seeing myself but looking at a stranger. The image in the mirror tells me that I am getting up in years, but I have trouble identifying with the woman I see reflected there. I may walk more slowly and be slightly stooped, but that is not the case with my spirit. It is as vibrant as it ever was. I guess that's one reason why I so enjoy reading all those romance novels.*

There are times when I would like to shout out to the world, The invisible part of me is not old! I consider myself essentially the same person I have always been. And so, people who are getting up in years must come to terms with the difference between the image they project and the self-image they perceive.

Recently I was walking on the North Carolina beach on a brisk, beautiful day and feeling remarkably agile and vigorous when I met a young boy coming from the opposite direction. As we passed, he waved his hand in a friendly manner and said, "Hi, old man!" It was a blow to my sense of well-being. I knew I looked that way to him even though at that moment I felt as if I were in my prime. Usually we try to cope with such discrepancies by the reassurance of that well-worn cliché, "You are as young as you feel."

Spiritually, the difference can be more easily accepted by remembering that God does not judge us by how we look. (Neither do the people who love us and are truly important to us.) What matters is not the outward appearance, but who we are within, and God knows us fully as we are. Thus, our self-image begins to take on a more affirming standard of reflection from a religious point of view. We know who we are, and God knows who we are, even though others persist in seeing us as being quite different from the person we consider ourselves to be.

Most people look better on the outside than they know themselves to be on the inside. And, of course, it is easier to work on outward appearances than to effect genuine changes for the better in one's heart and mind. As aging makes it hard to maintain the cosmetic facade, we would do well to give more attention to our inner life, dealing with such sins as self-centeredness, prejudice, and greed. It makes more sense to worry about the condition of our spirit than to fret over new wrinkles on our faces, and surprisingly, inner renewal often surfaces in a winsome and pleasing countenance.

The prevailing professional understanding of the aging process is that we move from childhood into our adult years and then through our adult years toward maturity, which peaks at midlife. After that, we begin a downward slope of decline until death. We convey this understanding whenever we describe older people as being "over the hill." With this perception of the way the natural process develops, it is not surprising that when we are no longer able to pass as young, we begin to conform to the stereotype and conclude that any ailment or debilitation we suffer comes with the territory. In other words, because we have been led to believe that decline is the norm, we acquiesce to it without question or challenge.

For example, occasionally I have difficulty remembering the names of people I know well. Whenever this happens, I assume it is normal for a man of my age and wonder if I'm beginning to lose it. I seldom remind myself that young people also sometimes forget names. A more serious illustration is the way the medical profession reacts to older patients who are diagnosed with depression. When people suffer depression at earlier stages of life, they get immediate attention, and treatment usually leads to a restoration of health, whereas, if depression is detected in an older adult, doctors often see it as a first step toward senility and may not give it comparable attention, although proper care might overcome it.

The fatalistic idea that old age is synonymous with deterioration and that nothing can be done about it is widespread. The English poets, W. B. Yeats and T. S. Eliot, both describe what it means to be old, and neither paints a very pretty picture. According to Yeats, "An aged man is but a paltry thing. A tattered coat upon a stick . . ."[1]

Eliot sighs:
I grow old . . . I grow old.
I shall wear the bottom of my trousers rolled.
I have seen the moment of my greatness flicker,
And I have seen the eternal footman hold my coat and
    snicker. . . .[2]

Such gloomy assessments of the last stage of life can also be found in Christian literature. Augustine says that, when life draws to its close, "the old man is full of complaints and with no joys."[3] And a part of the lost paradise that Milton laments in *Paradise Lost* is the joy and beauty of youth as compared to "withered, weak and gray" old age.

It is not surprising that well and active older adults are threatened by images like these and go to great lengths to distance themselves from such negative impressions. Nor is it surprising that young people think that the old are programmed to atrophy in every aspect of their being. We are perpetuating a damaging distortion of what older people are really like. Instead of focusing on the majority who are vigorous and alert, the word "old" conjures up thoughts of senile and decrepit folk who are warehoused in institutions. This image persists despite the fact that only 5 percent of people over sixty-five in the United States are in nursing homes! Most older Americans are still enjoying life almost as much as they ever did.

People who are pushing seventy and beyond are in a catch-22 situation. Not wanting to be associated with elderly people who are infirm and have disabilities, they make every effort to appear young and thus not be considered old as the prevalent image depicts them. Obviously, the aging process affects people in different ways, but most older people are independent, active, and in reasonably good health. Yet we have allowed the minority who are seriously infirm or have suffered reversals in early old age to be considered the norm for all of us.

When our task force began meeting to design the new Chapel Hill Senior Center, the question of for whom we were planning surfaced quickly. We soon developed an in-house vocabulary to refer to various stages of the aging process: the frisky, the frail, the fragile, and the fallen. (One woman was adamant that we cease calling the more active group "frisky," because she associated the adjective with her dog.) Our cellular clocks are not all on the same schedule, and so there is a wide range of differences in agility and alertness between the young old and the very old. Obviously, the way we take care of ourselves in the earlier stages of life may dramatically determine the degree of well-being we enjoy in these sequential stages of aging. But there are other factors that affect how well one functions along the aging spectrum. Dr. Linda George of the Duke University Center for the Study of Aging adds the word "luck" to her list, and others would mention genetics. There are, however, no reports of any modern centenarians having children who live to be one hundred![4]

Admitting where one is on the age span is further complicated by the arbitrary cutoff points used by various organizations to indicate who is included. The AARP now welcomes membership to people who are fifty and older. The benefits granted by the Older Americans Act begin with those who are sixty, and our society as a whole seems to consider sixty-five an appropriate time to retire. (One exception is the Senior Employment Program for which eligibility begins at fifty-five.) So, how old is old? For most Americans the question has a very simple answer: you are old when you can no longer function, are infirm, or are unable to maintain your independence.

The perception of age as infirmity owes some of its prevalence to the medical profession, which tends to see the aging process as a disease meant to be cured. Like Abraham, whom the Bible says was "stricken in age" (Genesis 18:11), many health professionals often see older people in much the same way. (John Wesley, the founder of Methodism, wrote a book on cures and listed old age among the diseases.) Understandably, health professionals who give most of their attention to those old people who are suffering from serious debilitating conditions may begin to think of the entire older population as being in a state of decline. And young medical and nursing students in a hospital setting may assume that the sample they see is typical of the group as a whole, which is a grossly inaccurate impression.

In order to project a more balanced idea of what the older population is like, our senior center worked out an arrangement with the nearby University of North Carolina Medical School to require students to come to the center to do trial case histories on healthy older adults. Students are paired off with seniors for a one-to-one thirty-minute interview to assess their physical condition and how they are managing their medical needs. The project has been a great success, not only by exposing young medical professionals to a segment of the population they seldom see in the hospital, but also in improving their communication skills with persons three times their own age. Both parties to this project seem to enjoy the interaction enormously.

Some people may be surprised to learn that current studies reveal that older adults in America rate their quality of life higher than those who are middle-aged and also higher than the young-adult population. This can be accounted for by several reasons. The older we get, the better the correlation is between our aspirations and our achievements. When our goals are more in line with reality, our level of happiness rises. Another reason is that most older people of this generation feel they are getting a fair deal. They judge society to be more equitable than the young do. Furthermore, older people today seem to have a greater sense of control in taking care of themselves and making their own decisions about what affects them. All of these considerations add up to a broad consensus among older adults that their quality of life is good.[5]

There are opportunities everywhere today for people to associate with older citizens: the church, the grocery store, the shopping mall, the neighborhood. Unfortunately, however, many people fail to take advantage of the opportunity, and the old people in their midst become almost invisible to them. Because of a lack of more direct contact, stereotypes of elderly people are commonplace, and there is a constant danger of discrimination against them. Ageism, the practice of relating to older people in demeaning and prejudicial ways, is ubiquitous in our society. Actually, ageism is more accurately defined as judging the worth and abilities of anyone by how old he or she is. Just as sexism imposes gender stereotypes, so ageism imposes stereotypes of elderly people. For example, a university professor who spoke at our senior center asked me as he was about to leave, "Are they always so perky?" His comment revealed his prejudicial judgment that generally older people are neither alert nor able to ask penetrating questions. And significantly, though I will soon be seventy, he did not include me in his judgment, for I did not fit his stereotype.

Because of widespread fallacious impressions of old people, many of them suffer daily indignities. Sharon Curtin in her book *Nobody Ever Died of Old Age* argues that ageism contributes to the death of elderly people. She describes circumstances that are by no means atypical:

> *If you look for an apartment, people may refuse to rent to you; old people smell and can't take care of themselves. If you stop to watch children playing, you're suspected of being a dirty old pervert. There are a million derogatory names for you: "old biddy," "crazy old coot," "dirty old man," "silly old codger." If someone wishes to pay you tribute, they say you're so young—considering your age. That is as grievous an insult as telling a*

woman she "thinks like a man."[6]

One of the most damaging images of old age stems from calling it second childhood. When this pejorative idea leads to treating an old person like a child, he or she may begin behaving like a child. How sad that this maligning stereotype often becomes a self-fulfilling prophecy.

I felt the sting of this association myself at a ski resort recently when I purchased my senior-discount lift ticket. Printed in large letters on the ticket attached to my jacket were the words CHILD/SR., indicating that children and old people were grouped in the same category! The old adage "once a man and twice a child" dies slowly. The issue here is our failure to distinguish between childishness and childlikeness. Jesus commended the latter and praised those who possess the openness, trust, and approachability of children. These are attributes we should all cultivate, but the word childish has pejorative connotations, and no one wants to be seen in this way.

Because of offensive ageism found at a nearby hospital in my town, an advocacy group met with the administrative staff to urge that sensitivity training be a prerequisite for all who care for older patients. Orderlies and aids commonly talk to older patients on a first-name basis, a practice that some old people feel is disrespectful. Others resent it because they think they are being treated as children. Another prevalent habit is for members of the caring staff to raise their voices whenever they converse with the elderly. They assume that if you are old, you must be deaf. In a current issue of *Newsweek*, in the column "My Turn," an elderly woman describes what it is like to live in a nursing home:

> *Why do you think the staff insists on talking baby talk when speaking to me? I understand English. I have a degree in music and am a certified teacher. Now I hear a lot of words that end in "y." Is this how my kids felt? My hearing aid works fine. There is little need for anyone to position their face directly in front of mine and raise their voice with those "y" words. Sometimes it takes longer for a meaning to sink in; sometimes my mind wanders when I am bored. But there's no need to shout.*[7]

All such erroneous ideas of what it means to be old allow little or no room for variation, whereas, in reality, there is probably more variation among older people than exists in any other age group. At ninety, some seniors are active and mentally sharp, while some sixty-year-old people are almost helpless. Isabella Cannon was seventy-three years old when North Carolina's capital city, Raleigh, first elected her mayor, and now that she is in her midnineties, she is still active in civic affairs. We are tempted to hear all such examples as exceptions, but we are guilty of ageism if we do. We can avoid it by realizing that individuals are precisely that, individuals, different from one another in varied and often unexpected ways. Several of the most alert and challenging bridge players at our senior center are twenty years older than the others at the same table who have trouble keeping the score. We do not age at the same rate nor in the same way, but if the medical profession continues to link aging with atrophy, we are likely to expect less of ourselves and become more dependent than we need to be. Though well-intended, many caregivers are guilty of what might accurately be regarded as compassionate ageism.

In light of the prevailing images of aging, isn't it strange that we talk about *growing* old? This seems an odd way to describe the process, for growing has only positive connotations. What do we mean by this? How ironic to associate the physical reversals of old age with growth! Our vision may dim, our hearing may diminish, our stature may stoop, whereas the word "grow" suggests just the opposite! This word seems strangely inappropriate to describe the graying of our hair or the wrinkling of our skin.

Could it be, however, that at some level of our awareness we see beneath these physical symptoms of aging and recognize possibilities of growth in other, less visible ways, perhaps mentally and spiritually? Could it be that the traditional model for aging as an uphill/downhill movement is false and that even our late years may be a time of a continuing uphill development? A strong case can be made for this. Betty Friedan advocates this point of view in her book, *Fountain of Age*.

Some physicians are also insisting that the time has come to introduce new images of old people. Dr. Mark Williams, a geriatrician at the University of North Carolina Medical School, teaches his students that an evaluation of the condition of an older patient is skewed if doctors detail the weaknesses of the patient without including notations of the patient's strengths and an account of how well the patient is coping. The emerging medical emphasis on health maintenance has the goal of extending one's productive years instead of simply accepting decline as the normal course of nature beyond anyone's control.

Aging is not synonymous with old age. Though aging may make us old physically, we need not experience decline in other aspects of our being. Indeed, in our youth-oriented culture, we're all so busy keeping aging at bay that we often fail to recognize new strengths that emerge as we mature. We have not adequately distinguished the physical aging process from intellectual development, creative capacity, social participation, or spiritual maturity. The ascendent/descendent curve is the model for biological development only. We should not assume that this same pattern applies to all other human functions.

For example, though it may be elusive to measure or to predict, our mental ability and sagacity may continue to grow as we advance in years. A number of recent studies have found that from 20 to 30 percent of people in their eighties who volunteer for cognitive testing perform as well as volunteers in their thirties and forties. There is convincing evidence that people reach their mental prime at different ages, some when they are relatively young, but many when they are well into their senior years. [8]

In many cultures old people are respected and even revered because they are judged to possess treasured resources of wisdom. Indeed, in our own culture we occasionally institutionalize this judgment by allowing very old people to serve on our Supreme Court. Justice Blackmun, at age eighty-five, just stepped down. Also, several recent presidents have been men whose ages would have mandated retirement from most other vocations.

Contrary to general expectations, some older adults even excel in physical feats. We have seen tremendous performances by older athletes in recent years, such as Jack Nicklaus in golf. George Sheehan started running late in life and became the guru for runners of all ages. A winning contestant in our Orange County Senior Games rode her bicycle all the way to the finals in New Orleans at age sixty-three, a distance of over one thousand miles. And forty-one veterans of World War II with an average age of seventy-two repeated their historic parachute jump on Normandy beaches to mark the fiftieth anniversary of D-Day—and did so without a single serious injury!

It may never be too late to learn nor too late to be creative. People who were far up in years must be included on any list of men and women who have made outstanding contributions to Western culture. At eighty-nine Arthur Rubinstein gave one of his greatest recitals at Carnegie Hall. At eighty-nine Albert Schweitzer headed a hospital in Africa. Grandma Moses was still painting at one hundred, and at eighty-eight Michelangelo designed the Church of Santa Maria degli Angeli. At ninety-four Bertrand Russell led international peace drives, and at ninety-three George Bernard Shaw was still writing plays. We could go on and on naming those who have reached their prime in later life: Arturo Toscanini, Winston Churchill, and Golda Meir. A current feature story in the *Baptist Press* tells about a medical missionary couple who at ages eighty-four and eighty-three are still taking mission teams to Brazil to treat thousands of patients. Though few people of any age excel to the level of stardom, ordinary old people can do extraordinary things too.

Achievements at advanced age can also be seen in the levels of spiritual understanding reached by many people late in life. Few of the saints were young but rather mellowed and matured with the passing of the years. Perhaps this more likely happens in the final stage of life because we are less distracted by the turmoil of adventure and the insistence of passion. In the quietness of being less physically active, we can be more hospitable to the Spirit. Silence and solitude foster meditation and invite spiritual companionship. Thus, we can continue growing in love and in our understanding of God. When we were young, our primary way of relating to the world was through activity, but when we begin to slow down, the field of action narrows and our hearts can take over as never before. The apostle Paul holds out this promise in his letter to the Corinthians wherein he writes, "Though our outer nature is wasting away, our inner nature is being renewed every day" (2 Corinthians 4:16, NRSV). And Plato put it this way: "The spiritual eyesight improves as the physical eyesight declines."

The quality of growth that accompanies old age may be significantly shaped by those characteristics that were typical of our lives during our physical prime. If, for example, you have always had an inclination to be generous, it is quite likely that you will become increasingly generous with the passing of the years. On the other hand, if you have been critical and complaining, there is a high probability that you will grumble all the more as you grow older. Miserable young people make miserable old people, and those who acquire the habit of happiness early in life are more likely to be happy late in life. The point is that personality traits probably grow stronger and become more definitive of our identity even as our body begins to weaken.

Caught in a culture that diminishes our worth with every sign that we can no longer be considered young, yet wanting to come to terms with our self-image as an aging-growing person, we are likely to feel highly ambivalent about who we are. One moment we play at being a young man or a young woman, and the next we project ourselves as a nice old gentleman or a lovely old lady. Surely it is far better to affirm ourselves as we are at whatever our age and to act on the conviction that we will not peak out but continue to grow as long as we live. By so doing, we will no doubt be much happier and will enjoy a sense of personal integrity.

The Scottish poet, Robert Burns, wrote the familiar couplet:

O wad some Power the giftie gie us
To see oursels as ithers see us![9]

A major problem facing today's older people is that we see

all too clearly how we are seen by others, and we know it is grossly inaccurate. Yet, sadly, we may still conform to it. It is far better to be true to yourself and to protest the stereotypes. You can age without apology. Old age need not be dreaded nor anticipated as a stage of inevitable decline. It is indeed possible that the older we get the better life can be. Reuel Howe had it right when he said, "You don't grow old; when you cease to grow, you are old."[10]

William Lyon Phelps, the distinguished professor of literature at Yale, spoke for many of us when he wrote:

I know of no greater fallacy, or more widely believed than the statement that youth is the happiest time of life. As we advance in years we really grow happier, if we live intelligently. The universe is spectacular, and it is a free show. Increase of difficulties and responsibilities strengthens and enriches the mind and adds to the variety of life. To live abundantly is like climbing a mountain or a tower. To say that youth is happier than maturity is like saying that the view from the bottom of the tower is better than the view from the top. As we ascend, the range of view widens immensely; the horizon is pushed farther away. Finally, as we reach the summit it is as if we had the world at our feet.[11]

Chapter 2

Experiencing Retirement as a Religious Crisis

Today it is not uncommon to hear people say they look forward to retirement, but many people who approach the end of their lifetime employment anticipate retirement as a major crisis, similar to a religious crisis. It is a time of self-examination and of questioning one's self-worth. Like a conversion experience, it mandates a new life and a change in lifestyle.

The prospect of retirement is threatening not only because it confronts us with some unknowns but also because the very word "retirement" has negative connotations. It implies that we are entering a stage in life characterized by a lessened ability to function effectively. It is as if you were speeding down a highway and suddenly have come to a full stop where a directional sign reads, "proceed with caution." From then on, you drive more slowly because you anticipate adverse contingencies ahead.

The time for retirement is not now as arbitrary in our society as it used to be. Not long ago almost everyone was required to stop work at age sixty-five. In many vocations this was set by law. The selection of this age as the cutoff time from the workforce has an ironic origin. It started in 1889 as a ruling by Germany's Chancellor Bismarck in a period when very few people lived that long. The chancellor chose age sixty-five in the hope that by then most workers would have already died, and thus, he would have no obligation to pay them a pension!

Today retirement practices in America are in an unprecedented state of flux. Many people are being offered early retirement because of necessary personnel cutbacks, and the benefits offered are often so enticing that employees say they can't afford *not* to retire. On the other hand, more and more older adults are working beyond their sixty-fifth birthday. They are in good health and enjoy their work and see no reason to stop. Mandatory retirement laws have been voided, and in many professions—such as university teaching—it is commonplace for people to delay retirement until after they are seventy or beyond.

Yet, in the minds of most people, sixty-five is the dividing age between those who work and those who cease to work. Social Security bolsters this mind-set by offering full benefits at age sixty-five, though, interestingly, Congress has acted to push this up to age sixty-seven around the year 2000. Even so, sixty-five is still the time when the majority of Americans concede that old age has begun, despite evidence that today's senior population appears considerably younger on that birthday than did those of previous generations. In fact, there is strong evidence that a person at age seventy-five today is biologically equivalent to a person at age sixty-five in 1960!

There may be advance warning signs that retirement time is nearing, but many people try to ignore them. These signs gradually get our attention whenever we hear comments that imply that we are beginning to look older. For example, the first time a hotel clerk granted me a senior discount without even inquiring if I qualified, I heard his unspoken message. I knew my age was showing, and I walked away thinking I ought to consider setting a retirement date. Or we start getting that direct question from new acquaintances, "Are you retired?" signaling the not-too-subtle conclusion that the questioner thinks we are old enough to have done so. (But, because more people are now taking early retirement, we rationalize that the question might not have been an observation of our age after all.)

The truth is, however, that others see more readily than we do the indications of our advancing years, and their comments finally force us to face the unavoidable fact: I am no longer a promising young man, or I am no longer a creative young woman. The reality check cannot be delayed. I can no longer deny that the accumulation of years has made a difference. Because our culture associates advanced age with retirement, the transition from the workplace to a life of leisure is generally tantamount to making a public announcement of something we might otherwise prefer to conceal: *I am old*, and it is time to retire.

A primary change affecting us at retirement has to do with our sense of self-identity. Living in a society that equates what we do with who we are makes it obligatory for the retiree to see himself or herself in a different frame of reference from that of the vocational role left behind. Our jobs may have necessitated spending much of our lives being what other people wanted us to be and afforded few opportunities for our associates to know us as we really are. At retirement we may begin to wonder if we know who we are as well.

After my own retirement, I felt increasingly awkward in not knowing how to identify myself. For thirty years I had told people I was the pastor of Binkley Memorial Baptist Church. I could no longer do this, and it was a painful loss to me. When anyone asked who I was, I explained that I used to be the pastor of Binkley Church. How relieved I was when the congregation notified me that I had been named Minister Emeritus! This new title enabled others to understand that I am the inactive former pastor of the congregation.

Many retirees face a similar dilemma, for after being introduced to a stranger, people often ask, "What do you do?" When this question came during our career, we had a ready answer that immediately enabled the inquiring party to infer vocationally associated impressions about our personality, our educational background, and our income level. But the brief reply, "I'm retired," conveys none of that, and so, when we are deprived of our work-related identity, we must define ourselves in unaccustomed ways. Thus, retirement threatens our very sense of personhood. We can no longer label ourselves as the butcher, the baker, or the candlestick maker, but must see ourselves simply as human beings. Just as the pain of accepting any loss in life presents us with a spiritual challenge, so may the occasion of losing our identity at retirement test our faith. We may feel we have lost our life and that we need a new one.

Who am I? is one of life's most basic theological questions. Others of comparable importance include What am I meant to do with my life? and What will happen to me when my life is over? Such questions at retirement may press with an intensity similar to a religious crisis and even evoke a more serious look at one's religious faith.

As we negotiate the retirement transition, a host of anxieties are likely to surface. We may wonder if the quality of our performance has slipped, noticed by everyone but ourselves. We may wonder if our colleagues think we can no longer pull our weight. We may wonder if our judgment is as respected as it once was. We may wonder if our production capability is comparable to that of our younger associates. The effect of all such anxieties has the potential for shaking our self-confidence and making us less sure of our strengths. We might feel under judgment, not unlike the self- scrutiny we sometimes feel during confession in a religious service.

We may also wonder whether we are getting accurate feedback about ourselves from those around us. We reason that the people who love us know what we want to hear, and that even though we may have slipped a little, they would be the last to tell us. This makes us become somewhat skeptical about the compliments we receive and causes us to suspect they carry a silent qualifier. For example, when someone tells me what a fine speech I have made, I question whether to take the assessment at face value or whether that person really meant to say, "That was an impressive presentation for a man of your age." A remark made to me by a masseur at the YMCA about the considerable agility of my legs illustrates this further. I replied, "I suppose I'm in fairly good shape for a man sixty-nine years old." But he quickly countered, "Delete that last phrase; you're in good shape, period." Yet, the older we get, the more we feel that the compliments that come our way are all conditional.

As I remember those final months leading up to my own retirement, I recall the festering fear that I had lost the ability to preach as I once did. Though I managed to convince myself that I functioned better in the pulpit than ever, I worried about content, anxious lest I had lost my reputation for relevance and my ability to communicate with the younger generation. I pondered whether I had changed or the world had changed and whether my perceptions coincided with things as they really were.

I hungered for compliments and waited for words of appreciation. When those church members who were closest to me began asking when I would retire, I was certain I had lost ground in my role as an effective leader. Maybe I mistranslated the intent of their question, but I concluded that their asking could only mean that I was no longer measuring up to the job. It was then that I determined to retire at age sixty-three instead of waiting for the standard sixty-five cutoff date. I felt it would be far better to leave the congregation while the majority of the membership wanted me to stay rather than remain too long and run the risk of having people dancing in the streets rejoicing because I had gone.

There is a related fear at retirement of disassociation from one's colleagues. Will they forget me? Will they be glad to see me go, or will they be sorry to see me leave? Will they seek my advice in the future, or will they judge that I have no further guidance to give? (Only once did my successor seek my advice, and that was about the management of the day-care center.) When we are made to feel dispensable, we conclude that we will not be missed, and our anxieties are compounded as we face the prospect of being isolated and alone. No one likes to think that he or she "can't hack it anymore" or is being "put on the shelf."

I dreaded losing contact with my supportive circle of clergy friends. As a retiree, I would now have leisure time that I would enjoy spending with them, but I knew they were occupied and busy. I realized that I had to proceed carefully lest I intrude or become an annoyance. Since I was retiring in the same community where I had preached, it was still possible to drop in at meetings of the Ministerial Association, but I soon found myself feeling like a fifth wheel there and ceased making an appearance after only two return visits. No doubt I was overly sensitive, but deference from former colleagues made me feel that their past relationship to me had been occasioned more by my long-tenured role in the community than by bonds of personal friendship. Subsequently, I have found that my main professional ties are with other retired clergy members. We like to talk about the good old days and evaluate what we see happening in all the local churches.

Obviously, one way a retiree could minimize severance anxiety is to move away to a totally new community, as have many of my new friends at the senior center. Most of these people settled in Chapel Hill from active careers elsewhere without looking back and seem to have had no difficulty commencing a new life in a new setting. But, for me, continuity of life with long-term friendships is an important value. I would have found it exceedingly hard to distance myself from all the people with whom I had lived the major portion of my life and to face the necessity of finding a new circle of supportive friends in an altogether new situation.

Further considerations surfaced. Would I be able to fill the vacuum left by my unemployment? Would there be new opportunities to prove myself? It became increasingly apparent that entering retirement was like moving to a new country—even though I remained in the same town—a new country where many things would be quite different from those to which I was accustomed.

Though the retirement event may occur on a specific date with a ceremony and celebration, experience soon taught me that retirement seldom takes place in a day. After officially making the move, people asked me repeatedly, "How do you like retirement?" and I always replied, "I'm not quite there yet." Long after you close the door to your office, you process emotions and carry an identity that is intimately related to your career. It is not easily nor quickly surrendered. No one can communicate to another person precisely how this affects you. It is a truly existential situation that cannot be experienced vicariously. It has to happen to you. You think you know how retirement will be and what to expect, but there are inevitable surprises. For example, on several occasions during the months just after terminating my pastorate, I found myself driving into the church parking lot as if my automobile were on automatic pilot.

A friend describes his first weeks after retirement as follows:

> *I felt completely at loose ends. I didn't know what to do with myself. I felt like a fish out of water. I ambled through the house from room to room, pacing the floor. I had recurring attacks of panic. The free time I had looked forward to enjoying was empty, and I made many false moves in an attempt to fill it. I felt as if I had lost all sense of personal security. I kept telling myself that eventually I would settle into a new routine, and of course I did, but believe me, it was one of the most distraught times of my entire life.*

A jarring reality that confronts one at retirement is facing the unavoidable prospect that death is approaching. You begin to feel that you are next in line for a funeral. Tragically, coming to terms with one's mortality sometimes leads to premature death. Indeed, so strongly do some people equate retirement with the end of their lives that they become victims of what is professionally known as Early Retirement Death Syndrome, as if one's perception of his or her uselessness hastens and abets a terminal illness. Similarly, sometimes when an older couple has been exceedingly close, the death of a spouse may spawn a decision for the remaining one to die too. I recall one such case where an old gentleman in his late eighties died early one morning, and his wife mourned, "I don't want to live without him." By evening she too had passed away. She willed her death. She concluded that her task of taking care of her husband was over and that there was no further reason to live. Two days later I officiated at a double funeral.

Regrettably, retirement seems to communicate the idea that one's life is over. Countdown time has come. Although the thought of our eventual demise may never have been far from our consciousness, retirement elevates its awareness to a more prominent place on our calendar of coming events. This leads to a wide range of possible responses: denial, depression, a heightened appreciation of life, and a possible deepening of one's religious faith.

The prevalence of depression among those who retire indicates the severity of the crisis occasioned by giving up one's public role in society. Depression, often referred to as "the common cold of psychiatry," is far more likely to be found in the older population than in the population at large. Professional counselors understand depression to be anger turned against oneself. But why at retirement? Because we feel robbed of our security and forced to make a new assessment of who we are. We begin to feel hostile about what has happened to us, and the negative emotions eat away at our ability to function. Our culture values people for their productivity and respects people for their positions of power, and so it is both traumatic and depressing to have the props knocked out from under us and not know where we will land.

As a pastor I repeatedly counseled people—especially men—who were plunged into depression after the retirement parties were over. Those upon whom others depended for executive leadership seemed most vulnerable. Some whom I counseled were suicidal. People who have spent their adult years in influential positions where their decisions controlled the lives of their associates often feel incapable of stepping down. They cannot accept the fact that their previous status and prestige are no longer recognized. It is as if their world has disintegrated, and they feel empty, unwanted, and worthless. It is clear that they find little comfort in considering themselves special solely on the basis of their being children of God. This basic religious conviction has been eclipsed by secular standards of value. Furthermore, once their driving vocational interest is surrendered, they may look back and question the wisdom of having given their lives to an activity that no longer affords for them a sense of purpose. For example, a man whose career was motivated by the belief that nothing could be better than making as much money as possible may now have second thoughts about how he invested his life. Advanced age tends to make physical assets appear less important, and when we realize the truth of that old adage "You can't take it with you," much that we have valued in the past may seem without value.

I like the story of the entrepreneur who was approaching

retirement and was granted the privilege of making a wish—any wish—with the assurance that it would come true. After considerable thought, he asked to see the stock market listings in *The Wall Street Journal* in an issue to be published ten years hence, surmising that he would then be able to predict the market accordingly and make millions. Miraculously, the paper appeared in his hands. As he excitedly turned the pages looking for the coveted information, he inadvertently glanced at the obituary page and was stunned to see his own photograph included among the deceased. This made his anticipated scoop look considerably less appealing. He then turned his thoughts to more intangible assets: his family and friends, happy memories, and his personal religious faith.

A successful retirement requires a severance from the past in order to more fully embrace the possibilities ahead. Ambivalence about leaving may tempt one to try to hang on even while attempting to let go. Some people seek to lessen the pain of a clean break by settling for a gradual scaling down of responsibilities, while others maintain the illusion of continuing by offering to be retained as consultants on call. But the inevitable cannot be postponed indefinitely, and when it comes, the transition resembles a religious conversion. For, like a conversion experience, retirement requires turning away from the familiar past to embrace a new life with a different future. If we have been truly committed to the vocation we are leaving behind, it will require more than walking away from it; it will require relinquishing the long-term emotional ties. Retirement does not really take place until we become detached from within, until we are liberated to look at who we are without our accustomed involvement and consider what new options now lie ahead for us.

In my own case, letting go proved much easier than I ever thought it could be. After three decades as pastor to the same congregation, I was not sure I could cut the emotional cord. Obviously, I still have strong personal ties there, but they are not binding to the point of making it impossible to remove myself or to take an objective view of subsequent events that have taken place. A part of the reason is that I accepted the challenge of another endeavor and channeled my energies on a volunteer basis toward the founding of a new senior center. This project enabled me to transfer many of my proven skills acquired as pastor to a new situation. I am still attending committee meetings, planning programs, and raising money. My wife says that the only thing different is that I don't preach on Sundays. I have closed one chapter of my life and am now in the middle of another.

Because people are living longer and some are opting for an early retirement, possibilities for meaningful involvement late in life now give retirement a more positive value. The sobering assumption that one's life is over is beginning to give way to the brighter prospect of extended years yet to come. Indeed, occasionally even middle-aged people can be heard saying how much they look forward to retirement, for they see it as a free and flexible time to do the things they are unable to do under the weight of their current workload. We might be more accurate to change the traditional terminology and begin calling the retirement years the elective years, for it is a time when people are free to set their own agendas and choose whatever they wish to do. Remember how much fun it was when you were in college to elect a course you really wanted to take instead of having to take one of those required courses? That experience may be similar to the pleasure you feel when at last you have the opportunity to explore other interests for no reason other than that you desire to learn about them.

A retiree who came to our town after a high-pressure career in public relations remembered the fun he had in high school when he played the leading role in a theatrical production. The demands of his business were always too great to include community theater, but as soon as Bob settled as a retiree, he lost no time auditioning for every Thespian event in the area. The male lead in *On Golden Pond* was made to order for him, and he played it with near-professional talent. He entertained many local audiences and gave considerable joy to himself as well. I have heard Bob say repeatedly, "I cannot remember when I've ever had so much fun."

Maybe the word "retirement" should be replaced by the word "refirement," for although our aging engines may miss an occasional beat, most older people can still function rather well. Consequently, today's retirees are insisting on being mainstreamed instead of conforming to the stereotype of sitting on the sidelines as a nonparticipating group.

For those older adults who have suffered a loss of their sense of self-worth, the volunteer movement is their salvation. It opens doors to where their knowledge and skills are needed and can be put to good use. I am thinking of the corporate lawyer from Chicago who came to Chapel Hill and became an advocate for the poor; of the surgeon who makes himself available at the senior center for people to "ask the doctor" about problems of personal health; and of the ambitious group of retired businessmen who put together a persuasive financial plan that made possible the founding of Carol Woods, recognized now as being one of the ten best nonprofit continuing-care communities in the country.

My friend Lee came to Chapel Hill after a business career overseas, taking early retirement. Having spent nearly all of his professional life outside the country, he wanted to get involved in the decision-making management of an American town. He offered himself for appointment to several boards and local agencies, beginning with the Department of Parks and Recreation. Having lived under dictatorships abroad, he felt he had missed out on the democratic process that so many Americans take for granted. Eventually, he tossed his hat into the political arena and was easily elected to serve on the town board where his business skills are now a valued community asset.

There are some retirees, however, who are not attracted to the volunteer movement and feel exploited by it. A few start second careers. For others, going back to work is mandatory to make ends meet. Fortunately, Social Security permits older people under seventy to earn almost ten thousand dollars per year and those over seventy to earn whatever they can with no restrictions. It is not uncommon to see older adults standing side by side with teenagers behind the service counter at McDonald's.

Your retirement is more likely to be happy if you began anticipating it at the high noon life, if you developed interests early that could extend beyond your employed vocation. Wise are those who have invested their prime years with an eye toward the distant future. For them the transition to retirement can be made with less stress and with a sense of continuity in the midst of change. Ideally, the process of moving into retirement should start long before retirement arrives. Just as we negotiate a long lead time to make the passage from childhood to adulthood, so should we see adulthood as lead time for the last years of life. Trying to resist growing old is as futile as trying to hold on to one's childhood, and failure to think about retirement before it comes compromises the possibilities for its best use once it arrives.

Some years ago, my wife, Pearl, who had a successful career as a musician, learned how to do needlepoint. In jest she told her friends that she was acquiring this hobby to get ready for her old age. I stumbled upon a cartoon that I took much delight in showing her. It pictured a little old lady furiously engaged in needlepoint, and hanging on the wall behind her were neatly framed needlepoint signs that read, MY CHILDREN DON'T COME TO SEE ME and I DON'T LIKE MY DOCTOR, et cetera—a host of complaints proclaiming all of the reasons for her unhappiness! Of course Pearl is not complaining, but my point remains valid: we should develop skills and interests early that will stay with us throughout our remaining years. In my case, a lifelong hobby of stamp collecting began when I was a boy. I can spend hours perusing albums and searching for issues I have not yet acquired. It is an activity I continue to enjoy in retirement.

Reference to my wife calls to mind another major adjustment in retirement, altering the relationship with one's spouse. Whenever we give up the routine work schedule imposed by employment, husbands and wives are likely to have much more time together, and this means negotiating new expectations of each other. In traditional household settings, a wife runs the risk of having her husband's management skills interfere with her established ways of doing things at home, and now that he is without a secretary, she may become his answering service. In many situations today, however, the wife also has a career, and frequently, the husband retires first and finds himself at home alone. The working woman's husband may then shoulder more of the household chores to ensure that his wife also has more leisure time so they can share it together.

Retirement can afford a wonderful opportunity to deepen a relationship and to explore one another's interests more fully. For example, my wife is an ardent basketball fan, and when I retired, I promised to go with her to all the games and travel to all of the tournaments. Her enthusiasm for the game is so contagious that now I am cheering with her. More precious than anything else, however, is the reassurance that can come from a life partner. I know my wife is "there for me," and her encouragement and support keep me going when I take on new projects. She also tactfully compensates for me in areas where my competence may show evidence of slipping. For example, she says she enjoys driving, but I know that one reason she enjoys it is that she is not altogether comfortable when I am behind the wheel! She also remembers names better than I do, and when she senses that I am having trouble recalling one, she prompts me quickly.

One of the myths of retirement that usually gets challenged before the first year of freedom is over is the idea that it would be wonderful to just do nothing and live a life of leisure. An initial good rest is surely legitimate, and no one should feel guilty for claiming such a respite. Some people can feel comfortable at this pace for years on end. Many retirees either play golf or bridge every day and never seem to tire of it, but most retirees who start out this way soon feel a strong need to be busy and often offer apologies if they are not. A question frequently asked of one whose retirement has begun is, "What are you doing now that you are retired?" The reply is predictably the same: "I am busier than I have ever been before!" Frankly, I suspect this answer may be evidence of a deep-seated need to appear active lest someone think one is lazy or irresponsible. It may also relate to a basic spiritual need to demonstrate one's worth against an eventual decline and a gradual fading away. We all like to feel we are needed and that the things we do are valued. One overly committed retiree said, "I am sure I will not die anytime soon because God has given me so much to do that it will take me forever to finish it."

News commentator Harry Reasoner is credited with a story about a man who lived on an island in the South Pacific where life is effortless. Each day there is a glorious sunrise, and one morning as the man walked out to the beach to view the splendor, he exclaimed, "Another perfect day!" and then he shot himself! This anecdote exposes a common discovery many people experience at retirement, that all play and no work can eventually become equally as boring as all work and no play. Endless exotic travel and every morning on the tennis court may gradually leave one feeling dispensable and irrelevant.

More important, Christians who are nurtured in the conviction that they are called to be co-creators with their Creator, to work with God in the ongoing renewal and redemption of the world and its people, may find it difficult to justify a life of leisure indefinitely. If retirees were motivated in their professional careers to see their work as a calling, it would seem a religious deprivation to do nothing worthwhile in the last years of life. And so, the question soon arises, How can I make my life count toward accomplishing something worthwhile with the years I have left?

It is no accident that in cities and towns across the country the construction crews for Habitat for Humanity include thousands of church-related people who are in their late sixties and seventies. Most of these volunteers are involved because they are committed to making our world a better place. They see the misery many families in America suffer by being forced to live in substandard housing, and Habitat offers an opportunity for people who care for the well-being of others to improve their lot. Senior citizen and former President Jimmy Carter is typical of countless older volunteers. He wields a mean hammer and serves on Habitat's national board.

Dr. Jitsuo Morikawa, who was a member of the American Baptist Alternatives for the Aging task force, expressed his theological perspective as follows:

> There is no such notion as retirement in terms of the purpose of God. [The whole idea of retirement at age sixty-five] is eroding, demoralizing, destroying the human spirit so that those who have not yet reached age 65 are already living in fear and trepidation. God calls us to live life with Him as co-creators, co-workers in the reshaping and renewing of human history towards the new creation. . . . and that calling is never completed until the day He calls us to live with Him.[1]

Fortunately, there are innumerable opportunities for older people to invest their time and energy in worthwhile endeavors for the well-being of humanity. At last our society is beginning to recognize the magnitude of human potential in our rapidly expanding elderly population. The majority of older people over sixty-five still want their lives to count and are ready to use whatever skills they have to leave the world a better place than they found it.

In his book *The Denial of Death*, Ernest Becker maintains that human beings need the discipline of work in order to be distracted from the ever-present prospect of looking into the void or contemplating their inevitable demise. Otherwise, he theorizes, we might all become insane. But, for the Christian, there is a crucial difference. We move through life in the faith that it does not lead to a dead end but to a destination. We see death not as a final curtain coming down but as an entry to a new spiritual realm that we can experience to some degree even in this life. It is a realm where our personal worth and work will all be validated in the final reckoning of God. Thus, retirees can face their last years without the paralyzing effect of fear, and, just as in those years preceding retirement, can be future oriented and full of hope.

Chapter 3

Questioning Assumptions about Spirituality and Aging

The notion that age draws our attention to spiritual matters persists within the church. It seems logical for this to be the case, for, as people enter their sixties and seventies, it becomes more difficult to avoid thoughts of impending death. As the shadow of death bears down upon us, ultimate questions become more urgent, and we seek spiritual understanding to diminish existential anxiety.

I recall an uncle who wrestled with alcoholism all of his adult life and brought considerable pain both to himself and to his family. At sixty he made a dramatic turnaround, became a devout Christian, and spent his last decade as an enthusiastic founder of a new Baptist church and as an effective teacher of a men's Bible class. It was as if he were preparing for finals.

Similar accounts of others who have experienced such transformations are not hard to find. Aging presses us to bring life into focus and to rearrange priorities away from material things to spiritual concerns. As a clergyman, I remember a number of older persons who made radical turns toward religion in their last years, and I recall others who were on the periphery of the congregation but who became more faithful at worship and more responsibly involved as they grew older. For a few, the church became the center of their activity. They were present every time the doors opened, whether for worship, Bible study, fellowship, or whatever. It was their life.

I am sure some of these responses were prompted by the unrelenting pressure of family and friends. I recall a man who asked to be baptized late in life, but I have always suspected that he did it more to pacify his wife than to affirm his faith. In small Southern towns anyone outside the church is targeted as a potential convert, and it takes considerable stamina to resist the evangelical fervor whipped up every year by the annual revival. Yet there are those who manage to stand their ground and not bend to the winds of pulpit persuasion even into old age. I have heard the claim that there are no atheists in foxholes, but as a former pastor, I can testify that there are elderly atheists on deathbeds.

Where does this leave us? It's dangerous to generalize about the relationship of spirituality and the aging process, but as I look back upon each of my pastorates, I can see the faces of those stalwart patriarchs and matriarchs who were indeed the pillars of the church. These were people whose judgment was respected and whose lives exemplified the power of the Christian faith to shape human lives. Though impossible to prove, it can be instructive to consider the proposition that spirituality and aging have a special compatibility. The assumption is found not only within religious groups but also in American culture at large.

In other cultures, perhaps more so than in our own, people believe that aging and spirituality have a unique relationship and that spirituality is especially prevalent and visible in life's last years. Someone has observed that the older Mother Teresa becomes, the holier she seems. This same observation could be made about many older people. Eastern religions exalt elderly people to a higher level of respect because they think older people are endowed with a clearer vision of divine reality and possess God's special gift of wisdom. Hinduism teaches that the final years of life should be welcomed as a time of spiritual vocation. Elderly individuals are expected to forsake the temptations of the world and concentrate on their souls' salvation. Renunciation of material things, retreat from active life, and disciplined meditation are more the norm for old people in Eastern culture than in Western culture, but a similar emphasis appears in nearly every religious tradition. Advancing age is believed to bring with it a more intentional commitment to spiritual exploration.

The association of spirituality with aging surfaces in literature. Shakespeare has a young man dismiss an older one, saying, ". . . old man, fall to thy prayers!"[1] as if this is the expected activity of the elderly. And Alexander Pope refers to beads and prayer books as "the toys of old age."[2]

Surprisingly, there is little in Scripture that attaches any special significance to the relationship of spirituality and aging. Even the much-touted length of Methuselah's life tells us nothing about his last years. One of the most pitiful descriptions of old age to be found anywhere is from Ecclesiastes, where the preacher writes with characteristic cynicism:

> *Then your arms, that have protected you, will tremble, and your legs, now strong, will grow weak. Your teeth will be too few to chew your food, and your eyes too dim to see clearly. Your ears will be deaf to the noise of the street. . . . Your hair will turn white; you will hardly be able to drag yourself along, and all desire will be gone (Ecclesiastes 12:3-5, GNB).*

The Levitical law commands, "Show respect for old people and honor them" (Leviticus 19:32, GNB), but nowhere in the Old Testament is there evidence of the belief that advanced age and spirituality coincide as a matter of course.

In the New Testament, we find the story about the old man, Simeon, who waited in the temple to get a glimpse of the promised Messiah, as if this were an appropriate place and posture for one of his age.[3] And there is an admonition to both old men and old women in the Pastoral Epistle to Titus to behave as holy people are supposed to behave.[4]

Unfortunately, we have no record of Jesus ever mentioning aging, with the possible exception of something he said to Peter as an aside in the Gospel of John about a time coming when Peter would be unable to take care of himself, implying old age.[5] All scholars agree that the disciples were quite young, and of course Jesus died when he was only thirty-three. Though theologians like to talk about Jesus identifying himself fully with our humanity, we cannot claim that he experienced what it means to be old. Regrettably, Scripture offers little advice about negotiating the last stage of life. It does tell us repeatedly, however, that God loves us throughout our life span, which may extend to "threescore years and ten" (seventy), but those who live beyond this can expect "labour and sorrow" (Psalm 90:10). There is no mention or promise of any special spiritual dispensation to face the final difficult years.

A likely place to investigate the possible correlation of spirituality and aging is as a visitor to the average church. In the majority of congregations, you would probably notice a high percentage of seniors. Nearly everywhere I preach I am impressed by the prevalence of gray heads packing the pews before me. It would be comforting to church leaders if they could believe that those who are now younger will prove increasingly faithful in their latter years, but there is no such assurance. It might be more realistic to worry about the future of the church when the current generation of old people vanishes from the scene.

Up until now I have used the word "spirituality" without attempting to define it. Although I am a clergyman, I must confess it is not easy to define precisely what spirituality means. No doubt each of us has some vague impression of what we refer to here, but even the dictionary has difficulty pinning it down precisely.

Immediately we think of religion with all the trappings of the organized church. Though this association is immediate, it is important to distinguish between spirituality and religiosity. Participating in an organized community dedicated to nurturing one's spiritual life is no guarantee that this will occur. You may be an active church member and not be very spiritual, and the opposite is also true; you may be outside the church and deeply spiritual.

The identification of spirituality with church activities is far too limiting. Genuine spirituality is never compartmentalized but permeates one's whole being. It is never narrow in focus. It reaches the outer limits of life and seeks to penetrate life's most puzzling and agonizing perplexities. The spiritual person is always open to transcendent experiences and stands in awe before the majesty and mystery of God's vast and varied creation.

A dictionary definition of spirituality as "the animating principle of human existence" seems cold and academic, but it points us in the right direction. We sharpen our understanding further when we acknowledge that spirituality is in some sense separate from and beyond the physical part of our being. It manifests its presence in what the New Testament calls the gifts of the Spirit, such as love, beauty, peace, joy, hope, and faith—values we associate with spirituality. Perhaps it can best be understood as the interaction between the human spirit and the divine Spirit, our seeking to hold onto God even as we are held by God. It is helpful to recall the biblical account of Creation, when at the beginning of time God breathed into human beings the breath of life. God created man and woman in the divine image, thus prompting the equating of spirituality with the Spirit of God within us. Although some people might not want to identify their responses to art and nature as spiritual, they are closely related to the same reality as sources of inspiration and aspiration.

A further helpful statement about the nature of spirituality comes from The National Interfaith Coalition on Aging. It reads, "Spiritual well-being is the affirmation of life in a relationship with a God, self, community, and environment that nurtures and celebrates wholeness."[6] Spirituality emanates from one's openness to God and influences all other relationships. It seems consistently related to the uplifting of life at every level of our existence. The spiritual person sees beyond materialism to dimensions of mystery and divinity enveloping everything.

When I accepted the invitation to address the geriatric conference for health professionals on the subject of spirituality and aging (referred to in the Introduction), I sensed an almost apologetic tone in the request, as if the medical profession had been derelict by not including a consideration of spirituality as a significant factor in health maintenance at prior conferences. This lack of consideration seemed odd because most physicians recognize that a patient's attitude strongly influences the outcome of his or her prognosis. Surely no one would challenge the conclusion that spirituality has the power to shape one's outlook on life, and in most cases, it does so positively.

Perhaps the prior omission of any presentation about spirituality by health professionals stems from a scientific mindset, which understandably could cause some people to feel uncomfortable discussing a dimension of reality that eludes scientific measurement and observation. Yet, given the evidence that spirituality is important to many older people, its presence should not be overlooked by clinicians as a possible source of healing and help.

No doubt a part of the reason older people turn to spirituality is to satisfy their search for meaning. There seems something intrinsic in all human beings that sets us on a quest for understanding our life situation. Basic philosophical questions surface early as we move through adolescence into adulthood: Why am I here? What am I meant to do with my life? How did the universe come into being? Where is history leading? What kind of creature am I? All such questions confront us not once but repeatedly, and they are likely to become more urgent in their asking as the years pass and if adequate answers remain elusive. Religion attempts to shed light on such topics, and the prevalence of religion in every culture is in itself evidence of the ubiquitous search for meaning.

Even though some people may not be in a position to make a deliberate choice, the place one stands in one's world perspective is nonetheless a subconscious reflection of our understanding of the meaning or meaninglessness of our being here. Our need to make sense of human existence may be more easily addressed in the later years of life than at its earlier stages, for at the end we can draw upon a lifetime of experience. We are in a better position to interpret from multiple points of view where we have been and what we have done.

It is not surprising that we become more interested in the claim that spiritual reality is the ultimate reality as our lives ebb away, for spirituality not only penetrates this world but also transcends it. This sets the stage for theological reflection, which few, if any, human beings escape. Whatever our age, we are always talking to God, even when we try to argue God out of existence. Despite the enormous power of the human ego, we can never ignore the fact that we did not create ourselves. Nor can we comprehend the mystery of all that preceded us or anticipate all that is yet to follow. With our modern understanding of the vastness of the universe and the intricate and dependable workings of the natural world, it is virtually impossible not to wonder about its origin. Whether we affirm God's presence or absence, we cannot avoid some consideration of where the world came from and who or what is behind it and why we are here on this planet.

Add to such reflections our likely eventual discovery that the things most precious to us in life are those best classified as spiritual. What meaning would there be in our lives if there were no love or beauty or joy? What purpose would there be in life if we were not motivated to work for justice and peace? Religion affirms that all such values are intimately related to God, and that as we experience and appropriate them, we are to some degree engaged with the ultimate.

When Swiss psychiatrist Carl Jung said that human beings would surely not grow to be seventy or eighty years old if longevity has no meaning for our species, he expressed the universal religious conclusion that life is absurd unless there is God. Most people cannot tolerate the suggestion that "life is a tale told by an idiot, signifying nothing."[7] We believe we are put here for a purpose and that we have a destiny beyond our brief years.

There is evidence that the search for meaning intensifies as we get older. One indication of this in our own time is the increasing number of older students who enroll in divinity schools. These are people who at midlife are convinced that life should add up to something more than a large bank account and a swimming pool in the backyard. They are spiritually hungry and think they may find a spiritual feast in a seminary curriculum. Whereas, in the past, churches generally looked to young people for leadership, I think they would be wise today to consider these men and women who have responded to a call to ministry late in life. The search for meaning that motivated these older students would likely ensure their being more mature spiritual mentors for members of their flocks.

Obviously, the search for meaning is not a primary concern of all older people, even though it may still remain an underlying influence in the ways they invest their final years. In Armistead Maupin's *Tales of the City*, Edgar Halcyon, a man approaching retirement, has been told that he has only six months to live. He struggles to cope with the prognosis, seeking help wherever he can find it. One day as he walks through the park, he sees Anna, an attractive woman, seated on a park bench, and he initiates a conversation by commenting about the book she is reading. The book is the Bhagavad-Gita. Upon noticing what it is, Edgar asks, "Is that the answer?" But theological questions quickly get pushed aside for romance. He and Anna make the most of the remaining months of his life by a brazen infidelity that seemed more appealing to Edgar than pursuing a religious quest.[8] This incident is relevant to André Gide's warning that "one must beware of the illusion . . . that the last years of life can be devoted to a more energetic search for God."[9]

We must also disavow any assumption that a higher standard of personal behavior can be expected of those who are old. I laugh when someone says to me in parting, "Behave yourself." I am tempted to reply, "At my age I have little choice to do otherwise." But I know this is not the case. Contrary to the belief of young people, there is no evidence that at sixty-five there is a cutoff point beyond which the world, the flesh, and the Devil automatically lose their appeal. Temptations may be less intense, but we dare not underestimate their latent power. Older people often make the shocked discovery that the Prayer of General Confession is as relevant as it ever was, that we are still "following too much the devices and desires" of our own hearts, and "and there is no health in us," meaning spiritual health.

Even though we may anticipate and welcome growth in spirituality as we age, there is no guarantee that it will occur. Nor is there any assurance that an energetic search for meaning will lead to profound and satisfying answers. Elise Maclay expresses her personal disappointment in the following sentiment from her *Green Winter* collection of word portraits:

> *I thought when I grew old, I'd grow*
> *Philosophical.*
> *People expect you to.*
> *Viewing life from a lofty perspective*
> *Would be a help.*
> *Instead, trifles loom large,*
> *There being little else of importance happens.*
> *Worst of all, I seem to be missing*
> *A lot of my old ideals.*
> *Help me to find them again, God.*
> *Or help me find new ones.*
> *I haven't worked out a real philosophy yet,*
> *And maybe I never will.*
> *I don't know.*
> *I do know that a couple of worthwhile ideals*
> *Are a big help getting up mornings.* [10]

Thomas Hood makes a similar wistful assessment of his spiritual state late in life when he writes:

> *But now 'tis little joy*
> *To know I'm farther off from heaven*
> *Than when I was a boy.* [11]

These voices suggest that the last years of life leave some people with a more acute awareness of their spiritual impoverishment than of spiritual fulfillment. Such people must find this difficult to admit if they are under the impression that spiritual maturity is expected of them. Hood's confession reveals a nostalgia for his more innocent years of youth as he realizes he has less spiritual substance to sustain him in old age than when he was a child.

I suspect there are many seniors who feel the same way, especially those who had the good fortune to be blessed with a religious upbringing but whose early heritage has been severely eroded—if not eradicated—by exposure to our materialistic culture. I recall a number of families who had exceptionally close relationships to the church but whose adult children now never darken the door. Their parents made every effort to expose them to the church's nurturing influence during their formative years, but for some unaccountable reason, it did not take. Some of these adult children reach old age with an acute sense of emptiness, remembering something they once had but have lost. To acknowledge what happened might lead them to feel both embarrassment and guilt.

Lapsing from faith may not have been intentional, but the seductive power of secularism shapes our lives in directions we may never consciously choose. A retired university professor said to me recently, "When I went away to college I put my religious beliefs in a drawer and left them there throughout my career, but when I opened the drawer to reclaim them years later, they were no longer there." He is not alone.

I read with considerable interest a collection of testimonials from celebrity seniors under the title *The Courage to Grow Old*. Nearly fifty prominent men and women reflect on growing old, with the wisdom and experience that comes from talented and varied lives. I was surprised to find only peripheral references to religion, God, or the spiritual life. Many wrote about the comfort and consolation they receive from the beauty of the natural world, but there seemed a consensus of silence against mentioning anything approaching theological conviction. I wondered if this was a tacit admission of atheism or agnosticism or if perhaps it indicated the reticence that intellectual and independent people often have about revealing their personal religious faith. They tend to regard religion as deeply private and resist the impulse to acknowledge or discuss it with anyone.

I observed a similar reaction when I proposed to the retirement community where I serve as a board member that it consider the possibility of employing a chaplain. Opposition to the idea was deafening. Residents wanted no part of it and resented the implication that there were spiritual needs in the community that were not being met. Again, I wondered if the response might be accounted for in part by their feeling that it was inappropriate for anyone on the staff to invade that aspect of their private lives. (I was also aware of a number of residents' being active in local churches where they might legitimately expect their spiritual needs to be met.)

Census figures are not available to document how many seniors in the over-sixty-five category belong to churches, synagogues, or other religious groups. Obviously, with the coming of advanced age, many who have been actively involved in these institutions may no longer be able to participate due to infirmity or confinement. However, there is every indication that religious feelings and attitudes remain very strong even though one is no longer able to attend services. A recent Gallup poll reveals that religious belief, and the comfort and happiness it provides, increases with age for Americans. By ages fifty to sixty more than two persons in three (69 percent) say religion is very important in their lives, and once they are sixty-five or older, the proportion who feel this way rises to three in four (76 percent). Only 8 percent of the population maintain through their senior years that religion is unimportant to them.[12] Yet, despite these impressive statistics, the mass media appears to be loath to show the practice of religion as a normal aspect of the lives of the elderly. Consider such recent Hollywood offerings as *The Gin Game*, *On Golden Pond*, and *Grumpy Old Men*. Miss Daisy of *Driving Miss Daisy* was portrayed as a Jewish woman who attended synagogue, but this was a rare exception.

In conclusion, as an aging pastor, I must make a confession. I am convinced that spirituality is not likely to be manifest in anyone's life unless he or she is committed to spiritual disciplines, such as the serious study of Scripture, the practice of prayer, and a regular participation in corporate worship. During my active pastorate such disciplines were built in, so to speak. My daily professional responsibilities required my leading other people in these practices, ensuring my own involvement. Now that I am no longer mandated by the church calendar to conduct Advent and Lenten observances, these special seasons of the ecclesiastical year are not as meaningful to me as I had assumed they would be. I miss the discipline of planning worship services, but now I am able on occasion to be absent without even a twinge of conscience. Indeed, I am beginning to understand how competing demands for one's time and the pervasiveness of secular influences can eat away at a person's spiritual commitment. Self-imposed discipline is hard, but it is essential if we expect our inner life to be sustained. Spiritual strength is available only to those who are positioned to receive it. As the Christian mystic Simone Weil said, "Our consent is necessary in order that God may perform his own creation through us."[13]

An advantage of retirement is having the time to set one's own agenda. We can be more intentional in nurturing our faith by including time for meditation and reflection in our daily routine. We can join support groups with other people who want to share a spiritual quest and with whom we feel comfortable in exchanging insights. Our reading can include books that interpret Scripture and offer guidance in spiritual formation. We can plan quiet days on the beach or hikes through the woods to escape the distracting noise and frenetic pace of urban living. We should be wary of too much withdrawal, however, lest we remove ourselves from the flow of life.

A personal indulgence that I consider a means of nurturing my own spiritual life is having added a solarium to our home, a place where I can cultivate and care for rare plants (bromeliads, cacti, and orchids) whose beauty speak to me of God's colorful and incredible creation. We need to pay attention to those things most likely to turn our thoughts toward God. Spirituality and aging come together whenever we put spiritual discipline in a place of high priority on our personal schedules.

To master anything requires a commitment of time and attention before we reap the rewards of achievement. This is as true for the affairs of the spirit as it is for any other enterprise. The church has a long history of promising higher levels of spiritual insight to those who submit to the teachings of the saints and are willing to focus on the presence of God. Often older people are more amenable to such a pilgrimage when the demands of this world begin to lessen and questions about eternity become more urgent. At last seminaries are starting to teach students how to meet the special needs of old people, but currently fewer than five divinity schools in the nation have faculty trained in gerontology. Yet, ironically, the first congregation many young ministers will serve may have more senior members than any other age group.

When I was young, I assumed that when people grew older they matured spiritually. I may have gotten this impression from my grandfather, who was the only grandparent I ever knew. He lived next door and was a devout man. He read the Bible to all seated at his breakfast table every morning, offered prayers before each meal, entertained visiting ministers in his home, and served his local church in every conceivable capacity. And he did so with great joy. When I began to age, I held on to my anticipation of deepening my spirituality with the passing of the years. I looked forward to a time when my continuing dialogue between doubt and faith would eventually end and my faith would be so solid that it would never waiver again.

But as I look back over my life, I realize that what I had assumed and hoped for has not really happened and perhaps never will. There has been no steady deepening of faith but rather a recurring series of peaks and valleys. I have learned, however, that during those periods when my faith is less fervent, I can count on its becoming strong again if I perpetuate the traditional spiritual disciplines even during the dry intervals of doubt. In light of this, I am convinced that there is nothing intrinsic within older people that guarantees growth in spirituality, but a continuing dialogue will always provide opportunities for further steps toward spiritual maturity.

One thing constant in everyone is a hunger for meaning, and this hunger often becomes more insistent when we reach life's final years. During the prime time of adulthood we were so busy that it was easy to be satisfied with short-term meanings. We were too engaged to give much serious thought to the big picture. I accept the analysis of therapist Elisabeth Lukas and judge her description to be an accurate report of what happens to most of us. She writes:

The main reason for today's desperate search for mean-
ing is not so much a sudden meaninglessness as a de-
layed maturing of our generation, especially compared
with our rapidly growing intellectual and technical
skills. It also means that every person goes through all
three phases: a general search for meaning, the discov-
ery of a single important meaning, and eventually the
realization that many meaningful tasks are waiting.[14]

Our general search for meaning begins early in life, and
for those of us who became Christians, at some point along
the way we discovered Christ to be life's single most important meaning. Then, perhaps late in our adult years, we
found ourselves facing many meaningful tasks that were
waiting. If in old age we proceed to apply disciplined efforts
to this unfinished agenda before us, our spiritual journey will
surely be enhanced.

Chapter 4

Developing an Agenda for Healthy Aging

As we grow older we generally take better care of ourselves and become more attentive to those practices that promise good health and an extension of life. People who smoke often realize as they approach their sixties that they cannot afford to expose themselves to the risk of cigarettes any longer. Health spas, which were once frequented almost exclusively by young people, now number an increasing percentage of older adults in their clientele.

Today's elderly people understand that it is not smart just to retire and take things easy. There is a sense of urgency about getting sufficient exercise. Many of us who in the past paid only lip service to such matters have started being more conscientious in our efforts to stretch our muscles. Earlier in life I considered exercise a good thing for *other* people, but now that I will soon be seventy, I am more faithful to a weekly routine of swimming. My physician recommended some regular thirty-minute activity as the best way to control both weight and cholesterol.

I also understand that healthy aging requires monitoring more closely what I eat. This has been difficult, for I love food and am compulsive about eating. I also have a long history of snacking, especially at bedtime, but now I take nutrition more seriously. I eat more fruit and vegetables, and though it is my candid opinion that most fat-free foods are lacking in taste, my wife reads the labels on everything she puts in our grocery cart—a task made much easier by the new federal regulations that require more intelligible information.

These are obvious and legitimate prerequisites for healthy aging, but there are other considerations that, while less obvious, may be even more important in perpetuating our

well-being. I am referring to our attitudes and the moral
principles we respect and practice. In short, I am referring to
the kinds of things we often associate with spiritual discipline. In the long run, these may make a greater difference
in how we age than how well we take care of our bodies.

Consider, for example, the teaching of Jesus that we "seek
first the kingdom of God." (Matthew 6:33, NKJV). I believe that
our health and happiness in life are intimately related to the
extent to which we succeed in doing this. The admonition is for
us to continue seeking and to set priorities as we do so.

As noted earlier, one advantage of retirement is that we
can devote more time and energy to the things we consider
important. Our professional careers may have prevented
this, but we can use our new freedom from the necessity to
work to invest more of our time and talent in things about
which we truly care. We can put first things first.

One of the most impressive things about Jesus is that he
always had time for people. He knew that we sometimes
forget that people are of primary importance. When the
disciples tried to rush him through the crowd and pushed the
children away, Jesus said in effect, "Not so fast. We have
plenty of time. Let the little children come to me" (see Mark
10:14). I am sure that one reason having grandchildren has
been such an enjoyable experience for me is that I have the
time to be with them. I let my ministerial career rob me of
the opportunity to have much leisure with my own children
when they were young, and I look back now and feel a little
resentful. Unlike most normal families, our weekends away
together were rare; Daddy was always on duty on Sundays.
Family had little priority in my busy schedule. Ironically, I
was always with people but saw little of the people closest to
me. As a retiree, I can to some degree compensate for my loss
by being available as a grandparent to my children's children.

It is more difficult to sustain family relationships today,
and if this is to happen, we must set aside adequate time. In
most families, relationships are complicated by divorces,
stepchildren, and distances that separate family members.
It is also becoming increasingly common for persons who are

over sixty-five to be caring for their own living parents. Longevity and the breakup of the traditional family makes the family tree look different now from that of an earlier time. Fortunately, old age often brings with it an interest in family connections. It is a good time for siblings who might seldom have seen one another during much of their adult years to reach out to each other again to renew the bonds of love that united them as children. Researching genealogies and planning family reunions are popular pastimes as we grow older. Giving more time to the people we love is an important priority commitment in old age. The affirmation of family support helps sustain our sense of well-being.

Prioritizing may also be revealed in our speech. One of the privileges that seems to go with senior status is the freedom to be more forthright about what we say. In some places of employment people are vulnerable regarding what other people think, and employees learn to be cautious and calculating in their comments. But aging brings with it greater autonomy and allows us to remove those protective coverings that were once required to maintain social protocol. Now, without fear or risk of reprisal, we can let it all hang out, so to speak. We no longer need to be circumspect. We can speak our full mind clearly and convincingly and share our convictions without apology.

Most people shy away from ever saying anything controversial, but if we are faithful to the concerns of God's kingdom, there is no way of avoiding controversy. I have seldom been known to tiptoe around any sensitive topic. This was sometimes difficult for me as a pastor, especially in the area of politics, because I didn't want to alienate the more conservative members of the congregation. But now, more so than ever, I say exactly what I think about anything and let the chips fall where they may. Now people occasionally look at me as if to ask, "Did he really say that?" Speaking truthfully may sometimes cause tension, but we diminish stress when we are true to ourselves and stop playing the role of a chameleon.

Søren Kierkegaard, the Danish Christian whose writings had a seminal influence on contemporary theology, is famous

for having said, "Purity of heart is to will one thing."[1] For
Kierkegaard, that meant seeking first the kingdom of God.
As we age, it is easier to discern the difference between what
truly matters and what is of no consequence, between things
that are of enduring value and things that are wholly worthless. We may find ourselves asking, "What have I got to lose?"
as we elevate some concerns and discard others.

Phillip of Macedonia had a slave whose sole assignment
was to awaken his master each dawn with the same re-
minder, "Remember, Phillip, you must die!" What a sobering
way to begin the day, and what a powerful impetus to put first
things first! Are there any elderly people who meet the
morning without remembering that death is drawing closer
with each day's passing? When we are mindful of our destiny,
we are more likely to keep our priorities in proper order. It is
a healthy perspective for living.

The Good News of the Christian gospel is that it is never
too late to reorder our lives and to give our primary attention
to things that matter most. Even if we have squandered our
early years, we can still give our best to priority concerns in
what time remains. Alexander Pope is credited with the
cynical observation that "when people grow virtuous in old
age they only make a sacrifice to God of the devil's leavings."[2]
Fortunately, God doesn't see it that way.

What should have first claim on our time? One activity
with merit is the expanding of our minds, or as some have
put it, "to think God's thoughts after him." This involves
taking time for serious reading to keep intellectually alive.
In an interview the aging, award-winning actor Anthony
Hopkins, said:

> *I used to have opinions about everything. I don't any
> more. As you grow older, you also become more ignorant
> in the sense that you understand that knowledge is re-
> ally a nuisance. People say that knowledge is power, but
> I think that when you have an opinion about everything
> you stop functioning.*[3]

Hopkins is aware of the danger of aging coinciding with
the closing of one's mind. Life's last years afford a unique
opportunity to get beyond having all the answers to a new

level of profundity, a level that sets our sights beyond the mundane to the ultimate. One of the most stimulating programs now available to older people is the Elder Hostel movement, which provides academic curricula for almost any area of interest for exploring God's world. Another priority way to be open to God's Spirit is to expose ourselves to the world's great art and music. All such endeavors that contribute to our personal enrichment also help to perpetuate good health.

A basic attitude that fosters healthy aging is rooted in the apostle Paul's understanding that "the things which are seen are temporal, but the things which are not seen are eternal" (2 Corinthians 4:18). Aging confronts us with the necessity of putting our possessions in a new perspective; it makes us face the unwelcome truth that at death we leave them all behind.

Though this seems so obvious, it is often very hard for older people to accept, much less to put into practice. As some people grow older, they become more acquisitive and more anxious about their belongings and financial worth than ever before. We are seduced by the false security of materialism most of our lives. It becomes an addiction. One reason old people cling to things is their realistic fear of needing a fortune to cover the cost of their last years, perhaps in a nursing home. This is understandable, but it is nonetheless important to see that our only security is ultimate security. I am not belittling the importance of careful financial planning; good stewardship demands that. But I am cautioning against the temptation to be obsessed with an accumulation of negotiable assets as if there were no other source of peace of mind. Spiritual sensitivity challenges the folly of holding things tightly and invalidates the idea that our security is ever measured by possessions, stocks and bonds, or money in the bank. This means having the faith to trust the future to God and to relinquish the seen for the unseen, the temporal for the eternal.

Healthy aging is more likely to happen when we cease grasping and discover the joy of more generous giving. Old age is a logical time to sort through the accumulations of a lifetime and to cast away the excess. Obviously, for those older people who enter their last years in poverty, this is not a problem, but even for privileged elderly people, determining what is excess is not easy. Now that most older adults represent a more privileged and even affluent group in American society, our consumer-oriented culture will no doubt continue to insist until our dying day that there are things we simply *must* have. Increasingly, older people are being targeted for marketing with unrelenting pressure because we are so many in number. It is not easy to avoid exploitation by the hucksters even at a time in life when our material needs should logically be diminishing.

Many of us have basements crammed with furniture handed down from our parents, and often our children have such different tastes from ours that they are not the least interested in heirlooms from another era. Of course, it is normal to want to leave things to our children, but sometimes they surprise us with the discrepancy between what they want to keep and what we wish to give them.

We contributed to a recent church yard sale a tattered, dirty rabbit doll that had come from my mother-in-law's home to our house decades ago. The doll was in such bad condition that we first thought we should just throw it away. Imagine our surprise at the sale to find it included among the expensive collectibles! Someone had taken the time to clean it up, and had priced it for twenty-five dollars! When our daughter saw that the doll was so highly prized, she concluded that she was about to lose a valuable family treasure, so she paid twenty-five dollars to take it back home!

Somewhere down the road, the majority of older people will move from their large house into an apartment, condominium, or a retirement community. There is little choice then but to dispose of one's accumulated white elephants. But it can be a pleasurable experience. I have greatly enjoyed taking box after box of castaways to sales for charitable causes. I have found special satisfaction in sharing books from my theological library with seminarians and younger friends in ministry. It was painful to give them up at first, but it made little sense to impose this task on someone else after I am gone. There is little likelihood of my ever needing them again.

You may make a surprising spiritual discovery when you part with the things you cherish, as Elise Maclay describes in her poem "Worldly Goods":

> ... It takes forever,
> Sorting things. I stop and think about where and when
> And I find myself thinking, I may have use for this
>   again.
> Nonsense. I don't bake angel food cakes anymore.
> Give the pan away. Funny. I thought I'd feel a sense of
>   loss
> With fewer things around.
> I don't.
> I feel exhilarated, free.
> Is this why You told the rich man to sell his goods?
> I used to think You meant to help the poor.
> I think now Your command
> Was meant to help the rich man more.[4]

In America the majority of people are blessed with an abundance of things, but the pressure to accumulate more and more makes it hard to realize when enough is enough. As we grow older we should arrive at a time when our cravings give way to the serenity of satiation. Already I am at a loss for an answer when family members ask me each December, "What do you want for Christmas?" I can't think of one single thing I need. My wife feels much the same way, though she still enjoys shopping when we travel, but nearly everything she buys now is for someone else, especially grandchildren. Gradually, we are acting on the conviction that only the unseen is eternal, and we sing with more gusto Martin Luther's powerful Reformation hymn:

> Let goods and kindred go,
> This mortal life also;
> The body they may kill;
> God's truth abideth still,
> His kingdom is forever![5]

As the hymn suggests, we should be willing to give up not

only our acquisitiveness but our lives as well. Jesus taught that "whoever loses his life will preserve it" (Luke 17:33, NKJV). This religious principle implies that we begin to die when we cease to make a contribution to life. On his seventy-fifth birthday, General Douglas MacArthur is credited with saying, "Nobody grows old merely by living a number of years. People grow old by deserting their ideals. Years may wrinkle the skin, but to give up interest wrinkles the soul." Healthy aging more likely occurs when our self-interest is balanced by a genuine interest in altruistic activities.

Older adults not only have much of themselves to give, they generally are eager to give it. But first they must feel they have something valuable to offer and are not being marginalized from the mainstream of society. Our nation is finally recognizing the enormous talent and volunteer pool presented by our burgeoning older population.

Fortunately, we are no longer locked into the nineteenth-century notion that old age is meant to be a time of disengagement. The federal government's Retired Senior Volunteer Program (RSVP) is evidence of a new perception of elderly people. Regrettably, however, efforts to offer older adults meaningful involvement frequently fall short of the mark, for often the assignments are not commensurate with the skills we possess. Indeed, many older people find it demeaning to be told they are needed and then to be given nothing more challenging to do than stuff envelopes! For a minority this may be enough, and, as someone has said, "There are no small parts, only small players." Yet what a pity to squander available expertise with make-work when there are larger tasks to be undertaken.

Another illustration of our government's gradual recognition of the valuable professional talent among senior citizens is the Peace Corps. At the outset it was a youth organization, but today there are 251 recruits over sixty years of age who share their mature experience in the Third World, where they can make a lasting contribution.[6]

Here at home, senior volunteers have become the backbone of many social-service agencies. In my own community they are essential to the management of the municipal shelter, the hospice ministry, and the daily distribution of food delivered by Meals-on-Wheels. An eighty-three-year-old woman enters all of the data at the computer bank of our Inter-Faith Social Service agency. Another seventy-nine-year-old woman works as the night supervisor at the community shelter for women and children every Monday evening. She confessed to me:

> I fight depression all the time. That's why I'm here. I
> live alone and have no family. This gives me a chance to
> be with other people. I was a schoolteacher most of my
> life, and that taught me a lot I need here to keep up
> with all these children.

Interviews with senior volunteers reveal an astonishing appreciation for the opportunity to work in such places. Although they are doing something important for others, they are simultaneously doing something beneficial for themselves as well.

A book published in 1991 titled *The Healing Power of Doing Good* makes a convincing claim that helping others is good for one's health.[7] This impressive study reports that older volunteers experience a heightened sense of well-being, increased energy, warmth, and actual relief from aches and pains. The relationship of altruism to health is evident everywhere. People enjoy doing good for many reasons, not the least of which is that it makes them feel good. The book reports that even such a widespread affliction as arthritis can be lessened by helping, for in the act of assisting others, people are distracted from themselves. Helping diminishes stress and eases tension; the benefits are both psychological and physical.

Nonparticipating people of any age who are isolated and preoccupied with their own problems are more likely to succumb to feelings of hopelessness and helplessness. However, people who possess a sense of the stewardship of life, who want to give what they can with what they have, are more able to bear their own problems because their focus is on what others suffer instead of their own plight. There is wisdom in that proverbial saying, "I complained because I had no shoes until I met a man who had no feet."

The new nationwide Communities in Schools (CIS) movement involves older people in the public education of children. Volunteer coordinators recruit in this age group for tutors willing to provide one-on-one encouragement to young pupils who need personal academic attention. Grandparents who are separated from their grandchildren by thousands of miles can fulfill their desire to interact with children by getting involved in such programs as RASTOT (Read a Story to a Tot).

Older people also find exceptional satisfaction in becoming advocates for one another. The popularity of such educational programs as Peer Learning, in which seniors who excel in a particular field of knowledge teach it to other seniors, is evidence of this. Older adults are often more effective in helping others in their own age group than anyone else. The thriving new senior center in our community was founded by local older people who banded together and took the initiative in establishing it. It would not have happened otherwise. Soon after the center opened, one woman said to me, "This place has saved my life." It had brought her back into social interaction with new friends and convinced her that her own opinions and advice are still valued. Advocacy seeds hope, and hope is intimately related to both one's spiritual and physical well-being. We find life when we invest our lives in the lives of others.

The political scene is another place where the involvement of senior citizens is mushrooming. In communities across the country, surveys show that a higher percentage of older adults turn out to vote than younger. A letter-writing group meets regularly at our senior center to inform elected officials how seniors feel about a wide range of issues. In North Carolina, older adults also convene a statewide alternative legislative assembly (called the Senior Legislature), to which elected senior citizens come from each county to hammer out an agenda of recommendations to be addressed later by state lawmakers.

Surveys of the volunteer movement in America reveal that over half of the people who offer themselves to serve belong to churches or synagogues, whereas, among nonmembers, only one-third are volunteers. Advocates of holistic health are quick to recognize this correlation. A sense of commitment to worthwhile causes is the equivalent of good medicine. A recent conference in New York of body-mind therapists attended by a representative group of medical professionals concluded that it is "reasonable to advance the hypothesis" that altruistic behaviors enhance the helper's health, although there is probably no one single factor to explain the relationship.[8] Just as the spiritual goal of disciplined meditation is to foster self-forgetfulness, so does offering ourselves for others lift us above the dangers of self-pity and despair. The concluding lines of the familiar prayer attributed to St. Francis encapsulates the discovery that helping others also helps ourselves:

> *Lord,*
>> *make me an instrument of thy peace.*
>> *Where there is hatred, let me sow love;*
>> *where there is doubt, faith;*
>> *where there is despair, hope;*
>> *where there is darkness, light;*
>> *and where there is sadness, joy.*
>
> *O Divine Master,*
>> *grant that I may not so much seek*
>> *to be consoled as to console,*
>> *to be understood as to understand,*
>> *to be loved, as to love.*
>> *For it is in giving that we receive.*
>> *It is in pardoning that we are pardoned.*
>> *And it is in dying that we are born to eternal life.*

Christian faith teaches that there is an inseparable connection between the journey outward and the journey inward. All that has been thus far commended will more likely happen among people who make a sustained attempt to nurture themselves spiritually, people for whom the traditional practices of religion are given priority. There is little doubt that such disciplines as prayer, meditation, and regular worship can be a major influence in sustaining one's overall health.

Pitririm Sorokin, author of the book *Altruistic Love*, stud-

ied the life span of the saints in both the Roman Catholic and
Russian Orthodox Churches. His findings convince him that
even during those centuries when life expectancy for the
population as a whole was short, most of the saints lived
exceptionally long lives. He attributes this to their spiritual
discipline and lifestyle. Sorokin makes a strong case for the
close relationship between spirituality and health maintenance, concluding:

> *This extraordinary longevity strongly suggests that not
> only is there a causal bond between sainthood and long
> life, but that probably the saintly way of life is a very
> important factor in longevity. Through the highest kind
> of self-control, through the deep peace of mind and com-
> plete integration of personality, altruistic love and saint-
> liness become truly life-giving and life-invigorating
> powers.*[9]

Furthermore, priority attention to our spiritual condition
prepares us for a healthy transition to the world of ultimate
reality, which the church insists is spiritual. The faith community believes that spiritual reality impinges upon, inter-
sects with, and transcends what we normally perceive as
reality here. Those outside the church occasionally say to
church folk, "You people need to get out into the *real* world."
I heard this often as a pastor, implying that the real world is
"out there" and not found in the sanctuary. I argue that there
is more reality, in the ultimate sense, within the worshiping
community than anywhere else. There we get glimpses of the
coming kingdom of God, and, by our exposure to the liturgy
week after week, we are more able to discern the difference
between what is ephemeral and what is eternal.

Most older people go to their physician for an annual
physical checkup. I did so recently, and, much to my surprise,
the doctor not only made his usual inquiries about how I was
sleeping and whether or not I was getting enough exercise,
he also asked me about my spiritual life and to what extent
I thought prayer and worship contributed to perpetuating my
well-being. As a clergyman, of course I gave him a biased
reply, but I went away from his office feeling grateful for the

conversation. I thought how wonderful it would be if everyone submitted to a regular spiritual checkup, just as we have an annual physical.

I even contemplated a possible list of appropriate questions, such as, "What motivates your life?" or "What causes matter most to you?" and "Where do you look for your sense of personal security?" The way we ponder such matters is surely relevant to our overall well-being. Questions like these become increasingly important as we advance in years, and they deserve a place on every agenda for healthy aging.

Chapter 5

Coping with Change

No other previous generation of people over sixty-five has ever witnessed such spectacular change as the present one. The world of today is dramatically different from the one into which I was born. Technology has changed our lives in unimaginable ways, so much so that some older people in remote areas of America feel like strangers in a foreign land.

Consider what has happened. When my grandfather founded the telephone company in my hometown, telephones were a novelty. Nobody anticipated its widespread presence, now even on airplanes and in automobiles! When I was a child, we had no television, and my mother cooked without a microwave oven and washed dishes by hand. Computers were unheard of then.

Consider mobility. Although we owned a family car when I was young, trips were never of great distance, while today interstate highways make it possible to travel with ease from the Atlantic to the Pacific without slowing down for a single stoplight. Jet planes take us anywhere in the world in a matter of hours—trips that were once harsh and difficult and available only to a privileged few. Now affluent senior adults have also discovered the joy of cruising the globe to every remote harbor, and space exploration has become so commonplace that we seldom even watch the liftoffs anymore.

When I was born, the world was also more static and serene. Life moved at a much slower pace, and though change was occurring, it did not seem frenetic or threatening. We who are older are tempted to romanticize about that earlier time and to look back wistfully to the good old days. A recent collection of published photographs from that era challenges this judgment by its title: *The Good Old Days: They Were Terrible*. Of course our memory is selective, and few old people would want to give up the comforts and conveniences they enjoy now for the way things were in their childhood.

Yet, despite today's technological marvels, we feel somewhat ambivalent about the new world emerging. Old-fashioned family values of togetherness, neighborliness, and good sportsmanship seem to be eroding, and we are disquieted by the violence that is disrupting urban areas as well as small towns and suburban streets. We also worry about the kind of society we are leaving to our children with its mammoth national debt and modern weaponry.

Though many older adults are future oriented and demonstrate remarkable flexibility, others tend to resist or withdraw from a world that seems more and more alienating. Change can be difficult, and what older person is not tempted to challenge all that is happening by comparing it to "my time?" We may feel that the world has passed us by.

One of the major tasks of old age is to learn how to cope with change, to move forward with the times, and to accept the fact that the simplicity of a previous period of history will never return. Our happiness in the last years of our lives may in large measure depend upon our success in relating to the continuing evolutionary change while holding on to a heritage that has made us who we are. Everyone, regardless of age, seems to have some resistance to change, and that resistance is likely to increase as we get older. But change is the nature of life. Sometimes it comes suddenly and sometimes it creeps up on us slowly, but, whichever the case, it is a constant force that few can ignore and none avoid. Unless we are open to what tomorrow brings, we will be left behind.

A part of the pain of aging is the necessity of changing places with the younger generation. We feel this most acutely at retirement, but it is a gradual, ongoing process throughout our lives. It requires considerable grace to move from center stage to the wings of life's theater and to watch members of the next generation take the bows.

For elderly people, change means many things, but its primary impact is felt most keenly when we are edged toward the end of life by those growing up behind us. In his perceptive

book *Learn to Grow Old,*[1] Swiss psychologist Paul Tournier
illustrates what should happen ideally as we age by comparing the responses of two former football players who have
aged out of the game. Both had been stars and had enjoyed
the adulation of their fans. Football had been their lives, but
now their days in the limelight have passed and new teams
have pushed them into the anonymity of the crowd, an
inevitable transition. One of the players maintains his interest in the game, reads about the sport, offers warm encouragement to young players, and follows their progress with
enthusiasm. But the other former player has quite an opposite response. He never watches the games anymore and
complains, "It hurts too much not to be out there on the
playing field." He sinks into bitterness and accuses the
crowds of ingratitude for having such a short memory of
yesteryear's champions. "Football isn't what it once was," he
says.

Not many things in life remain what they once were, and
here we see two very different ways of adapting to change.
We can withdraw and dwell on memories of the past, or we
can enlarge our awareness and be open to the future. Even
when aging limits our physical participation in the activities
we once enjoyed, we can still let our minds and hearts take
over to keep alive a connection with what is occurring around
us. The confinement of old age need never be complete in an
age when television brings the world into our living rooms
(and in a society more open to citizens with disabilities than
ever before, thanks to the Americans with Disabilities Act of
1990).

Stepping down from places of influence and power is seldom easy, but it is especially difficult when we look back and
see our accomplishments challenged and changed by those
who come after us. How tempting it is to say, "That's not the
way we used to do it" or "We never did it this way before."
Such statements smell of sour grapes. It just may be that a
new generation has better ideas than ours did, but even if
not, younger people need to find this out for themselves.
Instead of being quick to criticize, we should be ready to
applaud and be available for advice only if solicited.

Do you recall the statement attributed to John the Baptist at his baptism of Jesus? Up until then, John's ministry had been on the front pages of *The Jerusalem Times*, but when he met Jesus, he realized that his public role would change. Speaking of Jesus, he said, "He must increase, but I must decrease" (John 3:30). When we must change places with someone else, it's normal to feel an urge to tear that person down in order to maintain our lead position as long as we can, but it is far better to accept the reality of life's ebb and flow, which constantly brings new leadership into the mainstream to replace the old.

I am better at giving such counsel than in practicing it myself. When young seminary graduates were added to our church staff, it was hard to stand by and see them experiment with programs that I felt would never work. I justified my intervention by saying we couldn't allow something to fail. Gradually, however, I learned that some ideas that initially sounded off-the-wall worked remarkably well. I discovered that young people bring freshness and creativity to situations grown stale from sameness. Even now, my wife tells me I am difficult to sit with in church, for she senses how I react to every part of the service. From the liturgy to the sermon to the announcements, I critique it all. When we visit other churches, it is hard for me to change my perspective from that of the worship leader to that of a person seated in the pew. But at last I am learning to relax while those who are younger and have far less experience often do a better job than I did.

Changing places with the young also occurs when our children become adults. We parents are so accustomed to calling the shots that it catches us by surprise when we begin to hear our children telling us what to do. Slowly we move from that wonderful period when our kids relate to us as adult friends to a later time when they start parenting us as we once parented them. This too can be a pleasurable time, for usually this reversal of roles represents a new level of caring and responsibility on their part. I shall not soon forget when our son arrived at our door one evening with a car telephone in his hand, insisting that his mother and I should never be out on the highway at night without one. I doubt if I would have purchased one for myself, but it warmed my heart to hear Rob's concern for us and to know that he wanted us to have this extra margin of safety. Of course there can be a downside to such concern. At a time when one's self-confidence may be slipping in any case, our children's anxiety about our well-being may erode our sense of competence even further.

When I made pastoral visits to new mothers in the hospital, I often said to them, "It will take you twenty-one years to get over this," but now that my own children are in their midthirties, I know that you never get over being a parent. We always want to be protective of our children, and it is hard to keep silent when we see them about to make what we consider a bad judgment. It is particularly hard not to interfere when we do not approve of the way they may be rearing our grandchildren. But when we speak out of turn, we can cause considerable resentment. All such intergenerational conflict can be avoided by reminding ourselves repeatedly that our children are adults and deserve our respect.

I saw an elderly man being parented by his grown daughter recently in a hospital waiting area. She entered with him, and, after getting him settled in a comfortable chair, said, "Now you stay right there and don't move until I come back." After she left, the old gentleman turned to me and commented, smiling, "I used to say those very same words to her." This incident calls to mind Jesus' statement in which he says to Peter:

> *I am telling you the truth: when you were young, you used to get ready and go anywhere you wanted to; but when you are old, you will stretch out your hands and someone else will tie you up and take you where you don't want to go (John 21:18, GNB).*

As we change places with the generation behind us, we are more likely to adapt to the decisions and innovations of our successors if we interact with them and avoid the danger of isolating ourselves from their company. There is much to be gained from cultivating intergenerational friendships. For example, teenagers and older adults often discover unexpected commonality and can become mentors for one another. Both old people and teenagers worry about getting their driver's license. Both are anxious about an uncertain future. Both have doubts and difficulties with regard to sex, and both have recurring troubles relating to the generation in between—the adults whom teens call "my parents" and elderly people call "my children."

Life brings with it many losses, and they escalate with our advancing age. Some of the most painful changes we ever experience in life involve the deaths of people who are dear to us. Birthdays seem to come closer and closer the older we get, and the landscape of our lives changes radically as both family members and friends pass away, preceding us.

The loss of a spouse is perhaps the most wrenching of all experiences. It is number one on the stress scale and leaves the surviving partner facing an enormous adjustment. We are seldom aware of the extent to which our life's orientation has orbited around another person until we are left alone. Accustomed to relating to other people as part of a couple, it is bewildering to return to the lifestyle of a single person. Generally, men have more difficulty making the adjustment than women do. In fact, statistics indicate that widowers rarely live more than two years beyond their spouses unless they marry again.

When my mother died, my father's life was essentially over. I would never have predicted his inability to function after my mother's death, but he was lost without her. He never succeeded in forging a meaningful future. Instead, he succumbed to recurring depression, which led to psychiatric care, shock therapy, and, finally, to residence in a nursing home. Overnight I faced the necessity of parenting him in ways I had never done before. I had not realized how completely he depended upon Mother to structure his life. It isn't surprising that the loss of a wife or a husband often leads the bereaved one to withdraw from others, but this is the worst possible response. Socialization is imperative if there is any hope in transcending grief and getting on with one's life.

Aging also increases the likelihood of our losing other

people who are close to us: brothers and sisters, neighbors and friends, and even our own children, whom we always assume will outlive us. All such deaths leave one feeling empty and a little less attached to the world. It is then that we are in danger of allowing ourselves to be pulled into the past, losing all interest in the future.

In a special study by gerontologists at the University of Georgia, centenarians of that state were interviewed to determine the primary factors contributing to their longevity.[2] The number-one item on the list leading to a ripe old age is the ability to absorb losses. Think about it. By the time you reach your hundredth birthday, you have said goodbye to many people you love. These centenarians knew how to let go of their past and continue living despite constantly changing circumstances.

How do you do that? A part of the answer sounds simple, but its importance cannot be overestimated: you must permit yourself the freedom to grieve. The ability to grieve is one of God's special gifts. Until we learn how to deal with our sorrow instead of suppressing it, our lives will likely be shortened. Sometimes Christians say to those who suffer a bereavement, "You must be brave," and to some older people this means you should be stoic in accepting the reality of death whenever it touches your life. I am not talking about extended grief, such as consumed my father, but a period of mourning long enough to work through pain, which healthy grieving can accomplish. Only when we grieve over the losses we suffer are we likely to embrace life fully again.

Dr. Elisabeth Kübler-Ross teaches in her remarkable book *On Death and Dying* how the mourning process manifests itself in a number of sequential stages. Before the clouds lift, you may suffer a wide range of predictable emotions: shock, denial, guilt, and anger. At first it may seem impossible to accept the reality of what has happened, and for weeks after, you may proceed as if nothing has changed. Then you are likely to find yourself awash with guilt as you recall all the things you might have said or done, and you yearn to rewrite parts of the script now permanently in the past. You may even experience anger toward the deceased for leaving you behind, and anger toward God as well. In the end, however, you accept the loss, and the turbulent feelings slowly give way to a sense of serenity and peace. It is then that you begin to realize that life can and must go on. Grieving over the death of someone we love is the most challenging spiritual crisis most people ever face, and it will occur with more frequency the older we get.

Change brings other losses that can hurt about as much as the loss of people we love. When we enter our last years, it becomes increasingly difficult and eventually impossible to keep alive some of the dreams and ambitions that had been foremost in our thoughts during the peak of our career. We must come to terms with the hard reality that the achievements we had planned to make, the promotions we expected to get, and the windfalls that were to come our way will never happen. We may suffer acute disappointment and even humiliation as we grieve for what might have been but never was. We may come to the end of our lives feeling like Willie Loman in *Death of a Salesman*, who finally could deceive himself no longer about someday becoming successful.

Further losses that are common among older people are physical deprivations. The loss of teeth, the dimming of sight, the fading of sound, the loss of sexual potency—most of these are prevalent among the very old. Such changes may force us to see ourselves in a different light and may demand that we relate to the world in new ways. Yet the ability of many persons with visual and hearing disabilities to accept their loss is truly astonishing. I am thinking of a neighbor whose sight was taken from her within six short months, so quickly that she had no opportunity to ameliorate her loss by learning adaptive skills such as braille. Yet, without ever a complaint, Frances accepted this unwelcome change and enriches her days in knitting, listening to recorded books, socializing with friends over the telephone, and even riding in the cart with her husband around the golf course. She never indulges in self-pity but speaks with appreciation for the blessings she has. Her ability to face each day illustrates the claim that, though losses are legitimate occasions for grief, they may also be occasions for spiritual growth. Equally impressive is the faithful care and attentiveness of her husband. Many older husbands and wives can someday expect to play such a role for their spouse.

One physical loss seldom about talked either in private or public is the diminishing of one's sexual function. Until the present generation, it was generally assumed that there was not much sexual activity among older people. Recent studies reveal just the opposite. There are wide variations in attitudes toward sex among senior adults, and, here again, most older people are victims of societal conditioning. We have been led to anticipate a waning of sexual interest, but if our own experience teaches otherwise, we are reticent and perhaps embarrassed to admit it. Older people think that young people see sexual activity as an inappropriate geriatric pleasure, but at whatever one's age, intimacy is a fundamental human need, and touching is a way to express it. Sexuality is always more than genital. (A sex therapist at our senior center remarked that sex is more related to what happens between the ears than to what happens between the legs.)

Although diseases associated with aging may diminish sexual potency, modern medicine offers a wide range of treatments to improve one's sexual capability, but unfortunately, the subject is so taboo for most older adults that they hesitate to talk about it with their physician. Thus, they are vulnerable to mourning a loss that need not have occurred.

Few things are more upsetting to older people than the necessity of surrendering their driver's licenses. After a lifetime of mobility, it is traumatic to be told you can no longer have access to an automobile. Nothing in our culture more dramatically symbolizes the loss of independence than an inability to hit the road at will. This is a touchy subject, for most states are surprisingly lenient in granting licenses to even the very old, but public pressure is rising to halt the practice. Heated arguments and deep resentments arise when children intervene and insist that their parents cease driving. They feel—and no doubt quite rightly most of the time—that the risk of an accident is too high to indulge this convenience. Wise are those older people who also recognize the danger and realize when the time has come to catch the

bus. (The AARP addresses this dilemma by offering "Fifty-
five Alive" classes that teach older drivers how to avoid the
most common accidents.)

Theologian Reinhold Niebuhr is credited with composing
the classic prayer, "Lord, give me the courage to change the
things I can change, to accept the things I cannot change, and
the wisdom to know the difference." Aging confronts us with
multiple losses that we cannot change, but if we are smart
enough to see that our only choice is to adapt to them, our
lives will be extended and our stress diminished. The findings
of the Georgia centenarian study strongly document this
claim.

In order to sensitize caregivers to the range of potential
losses that many older people endure in their last years, the
Ethics Committee of the Carol Woods Retirement Community provides workshops for members of the health-center
staff. At the last one I attended, the leader asked everyone
present to list the five most precious things in his or her life
and to write them on slips of paper, numbering the slips from
one to five in order of their importance—such things as one's
children, one's spouse, one's health, one's home, et cetera.
Then the leader asked everyone to crumple and cast aside
number three. The staff was told that most of the patients
they work with have long since had to survive without whatever number three represented. In a continuing sequence, the
participants were asked to destroy each of the remaining
slips of paper, symbolizing the loss of the most cherished
things in their lives. It was a graphic exercise intended to
enable the staff to identify with changes their patients had
been forced to accept in their last years.

Fortunately, many of the changes we fear never material-
ize, yet one of the perils of aging is to worry about losses that
might lie ahead. Although we should not be derelict in planning for all possible contingencies, we should also not worry
ourselves to death about events that could happen but may
not. There is a story about a man whose wife was always
anxious about their house being broken into by a burglar.
Throughout their married life she had repeatedly awakened

him in the middle of the night to go downstairs and investigate a noise she heard. The scenario was always the same. He checked everywhere, found nothing, and came back to bed. Then, one night as they enacted the familiar routine, the husband sleepily made his way down the steps and was shocked to find himself standing face-to-face with an intruder. He extended his hand and introduced himself and said he would give to the burglar anything he wanted in return for just one favor: would he please follow him upstairs to meet his wife who had been looking for him for forty years!

The things we fear do not always occur, but worry may nonetheless cripple one's life. In that familiar New Testament story about Jesus' visit at the home of the two sisters, Jesus said to Martha, "You are worried and anxious about many things, but . . . only one thing is needed" (Luke 10:41, Goodspeed) And what is the one thing needed? His answer may sound simplistic, for in effect, Jesus said, "You need to listen to me." He taught that most of our worries are unwarranted. "Look at the wild birds. . . . Your heavenly Father feeds them. Are you not of more account than they?" Then Jesus exclaimed, "You who have so little faith!" (Matthew 6:26,30, Goodspeed).

Faith is a strong antidote to worry. Let me illustrate. Recently, I endured one of those weeks when everything seemed to go wrong. I was pressed on every side and worried about how I would possibly meet all the deadlines to which I had committed myself. Then the unexpected happened, which brought everything to a sudden halt. There was a death in my family, and I was faced with the necessity of dropping everything in order to attend the funeral in my hometown over five hours away. The next day as I sat in the quietness of the church and listened to the minister read those reassuring words of Jesus, "Let not your heart be troubled; you believe in God, believe also in Me" (John 14:1, NKJV). I began to experience a sense of inward calm. My hurried life appeared less pressing. I began to see it all from a new perspective and to put my mind back within a framework of religious faith. I had been "worried and anxious about many things" but had neglected the one thing I needed most, attention to my spiritual state. The funeral forced me to be still and to remember that I am a contingent being, wholly dependent upon God's goodness and grace. Faith is the spiritual gift that enables us to act in the conviction that God is also acting with us. It is the ability to trust God as our ally and advocate in every situation.

Another major change eventually faced by most older people is a move from where they live into a scaled-down living situation. Pulling up roots is seldom easy, and often older people do not transplant as readily as younger people. Conditioned as elderly people are to anticipate the possibility of imminent physical decline, those who have made it beyond their sixties soon begin to ponder with a mounting sense of urgency where they should spend their last years.

People who have lived in many different places during their lifetime may not find the prospect of moving too difficult in itself, but this last move is unlike any move that has preceded it. It brings with it an entirely new set of considerations, for this is a decision that must be made in the awareness of a wide range of scenarios. We weigh the alternatives and look as far down the road as possible to foresee every conceivable contingency. Yet, in the final analysis, whatever choice we make is to some degree a gamble.

No one can be certain in advising another as to what is best. People who have lived in cold wintry climates may decide to head south where there is no snow to shovel. Others may crave continuity in their lives and choose to remain in their same area, either by running the risk of staying in their own homes or entering a retirement community nearby. For people with adequate resources, a continuing-care facility may look appealing because it promises lifetime security and protects children from the possible necessity of caring for them. It also appeals to couples because it removes the worry about who would care for the remaining spouse. Other seniors may have little choice but to live with their children, while some may move to a totally new place just to be near a son or daughter. (Those who do this often get left behind in a strange town because their children later accept employment elsewhere.) At best, whatever we do is an act of faith. Just like Abraham and Sarah, summoned by God to leave their home and settle in a new place without being able to see the changes in store, so too do many older Americans move from one place to another today.

My wife and I have no desire to live anywhere other than where we live now, but we have put our names on a waiting list at the nearby Carol Woods Retirement Community. We fret about when we should make the big move, and as each year passes, we wonder if we are pushing our luck by choosing to make the transition later rather than sooner. I find it very hard to contemplate moving out of the house we love and giving up the yard I have tended for more than twenty years. It is as if I am hoping for a reprieve. I have not forgotten how painful it was to close the door to my parents' home for the last time when I put it up for sale years ago. I was consumed with nostalgia for weeks afterward as I recalled all the family memories associated with that house, and now I am already experiencing similar feelings in advance as we consider closing the door on our home. Yet, I am convinced of the wisdom of the impending change not only because of the increasing burden of maintaining a large house but also because of the built-in security of continuing health care at the retirement complex. When the time comes to be uprooted, I hope I can look forward to the challenge and survive the transition without looking back. If we view life as a spiritual journey, we can be consoled by our faith that God always goes before us.

It is important for older adults to make such plans for themselves while they are able to consider the alternatives. The temptation is to delay making them indefinitely until some crisis occurs. As one old gentleman put it, "When you get to be eighty, it's time to begin planning ahead." It is better to do it later than never, but it is better never late. Otherwise, plans may be imposed upon you without your consent. I have a friend who could not bear the thought of ever leaving her home, but her children did not approve and arrived unannounced one weekend to move her to an institution she had never seen in a city far away from her friends. Not surprisingly, she has been miserable in the new situation and has lingering resentment toward her children for forcing this upon her against her will. The choice was made for the convenience of the children who had little patience with the strong emotional resistance of their mother. The way to prevent such a tragedy is to take the initiative yourself, put things in writing (perhaps even with a lawyer), and do this sufficiently early, lest relatives move into the void and make the decision for you.

Because of the high cost of most retirement communities and because many older people do not want to be confined to what they consider a ghetto of the aged, other innovative living arrangements for elderly people are gaining a following. In my town several local churches purchased a commodious house that is known as Share-a-Home. It is available to older people who do not want to live alone but who elect to share with several others a homelike setting. All residents split expenses and together employ a homemaker to manage the facility and supervise meal preparation. The cost of this arrangement is much less than most forms of institutional living. Another experiment, also present in my town, is the cooperative-community concept. In this case, a number of people—couples, singles, families, young and old—pool their resources and simultaneously construct private residences for everyone, along with common living areas. This method uses architecture as a catalyst for community, and it is intentionally intergenerational, always including some older people whom other residents welcome as members of their extended family.

Now that a major emphasis in contemporary medicine is community-based health-care delivery, many older adults hope to stay right where they are and depend upon home health agencies to make services available on a visitation basis. Though this may seem to promise less expense than to be in a nursing home, this in fact may not be the case. If you calculate the cost of nursing-home care, it averages about four dollars per hour, less than you would pay a sitter.

Another creative option for senior adults who have disabilities or impairments and who live with family members who are still on a nine-to-five workday is adult day care. Most communities now have facilities that provide a place for aging people to stay during the day while the other members of their households are away. A family member takes them to the center in the morning as he or she leaves for work and then picks them up in the afternoon when the workday is over. (There is some objection to the childlike associations of the name "adult day care," but an alternative name has not yet surfaced.)

Obviously, the choice one makes depends upon one's particular needs and the financial resources available. What is best for one may not be at all suitable for another. Betty Friedan makes a strong case against settling in enclaves of older people, such as the Florida scene or Arizona's Sun City. She believes there is great benefit in older people's retaining intergenerational and community ties wherever possible. Though fear of loneliness in the final years or dread of ending up in a nursing home may prompt people to sign on the dotted line for a continuing-care facility, it is wise to guard against being cut off from the community at large. Much-needed stimulation from outside can cushion the trauma of adjusting to residence in an institution. An affiliation with a local church is an obvious way to forge local friendships beyond the retirement-village fence. I recall a woman who moved from New England to become a resident at Carol Woods, but, for a year previous, she rented an apartment in town and joined our church. She recognized the importance of relating to the larger community first and saw the danger of confining her activities to the retirement-home campus.

Despite the best-laid plans, the living arrangements for one's last years may bring serendipities and unpredictable change. I am thinking of a professional woman who had never married and who upon retirement purchased an apartment in a nearby retirement village, thinking this would be her residence all her remaining years. But when a man she had dated as a young girl learned that she was alive, he came seeking her hand in marriage. He persuaded her to leave the retirement home and move some distance away to share their final years. Never have I officiated at a more joyful wedding, as a full church witnessed the eighty-two-year-old bride walk down the aisle. She and her groom have had five wonderful years keeping house together. She accepted the challenge of a major change late in life and is quick to say, "He was worth waiting for."

An African American couple who retired to Chapel Hill also comes to mind. Ten years ago they came from eastern North Carolina where each had had a major role as a leader in the community, but, because of the legacy of segregation, they had associated primarily with black people there. In Chapel Hill they bought a home in a neighborhood surrounded by white families and joined our predominately white congregation. They had the courage to carve out an altogether different lifestyle in their last years. Mabel and Bill made friends readily and became so integrally involved in the church that they were the first couple in its history to be elected on the same ballot to serve as deacons. These last years have been among their happiest. They know how to cope with change.

Imagine what life would be like if everything were predictable. Suppose we always knew what the future held. Despite its uncertainty and its losses, I believe we would prefer life as it is. Though older people are often stereotyped as being set in their ways, there is abundant evidence that most adapt to change remarkably well.

I am sure religious faith is a major influence in steadying our lives. In the midst of all the vicissitudes we experience, if we believe in God, we feel the security of being related to Someone who never changes and who meets us in every circumstance, both good and bad. It is understandable that one of the most frequently prayed prayers of the very old is, "O thou, who changest not, abide with me."

Chapter 6

Avoiding an Obsession with Health

It is surprising that anyone in America escapes the temptation of becoming obsessed with health. It is not surprising that older people are more susceptible to this danger and frequently give their attention to little else.

At every commercial break on television, ads inform us of some remedy for every possible ache or pain. Over-the-counter drugs are readily available everywhere, now standard stock even in grocery stores. Every day on the evening news there is nearly always a feature about some medical breakthrough or advice for people suffering from one ailment or another. Magazines include articles about ways to improve our health, and there are frequent feature stories about individuals battling some bizarre disease.

Health maintenance is at the top of the agenda of senior-adult concerns, and the wellness program is a major attraction at most senior centers. Health screenings, blood pressure checks, flu shots, and presenters about nearly every possible health problem are available on a daily basis. Another drawing card is the multiple exercise and aerobic classes pitched at various levels of strenuousness, including T'ai Chi and the now popular line dancing. Physical fitness is a primary objective for elderly people, just as it is for the young.

The goal is commendable, for it is plain common sense to perpetuate good health. The trouble is, however, that there is so much information to be absorbed about what is good for you and what is not that it becomes almost a full-time job to track the latest word from medical and pharmaceutical authorities. Health fads come and go. What was considered mandatory yesterday may be judged optional or even harmful tomorrow.

This is especially the case in the area of weight management, dieting, and establishing good eating habits. Monitoring caloric and fat intake is a never-ending task. You must read all the fine print on every label in the supermarket, and even after doing so, you may be left with a lingering suspicion that you still don't have sufficient knowledge to make the best selection of food. The old-fashioned breakfast of eggs and bacon, which was once standard fare for almost everyone, is fast becoming extinct. Yogurt is replacing ice cream, and substitute sweeteners compete with sugar on all restaurant tables.

Advice about what we eat is so bewildering that sometimes it would seem easier just to abstain from food altogether. The cholesterol scare has been a constant worry, but then there's an article in *Atlantic* magazine that tells us that our cholesterol count is irrelevant if we are elderly and that good cholesterol readings may not extend one's life more than several months at the most.[1] Research now shows that choosing margarine as a healthful alternative to butter has been a serious mistake and that we are better off to stay with butter after all. A news story announces scientific evidence that vitamins C and E can lengthen one's life, but in order to meet the minimum standards required, one would have to eat the equivalent of twenty-five oranges per day and six cups of almonds! But a front page story in *The New York Times* invites us to rejoice in the discovery that we can consume valentine chocolates with a clear conscience because, although chocolate is rich in fat, it miraculously spares blood vessels and will not stop the beat of our fluttering hearts![2]

Attempts to keep people informed about current health-care findings have spawned countless periodicals and newsletters, such as *Prevention Magazine*, all aimed at giving the latest advice about how to take care of oneself. This well-intended mission may inadvertently be responsible for starting a mass neurosis: an obsession with health.

I like the anecdote about the woman who was asked by her friend, "How are you?" to which she replied, "How soon do you have to know?" Her response suggests the kind of protracted uncertainty so prevalent among older people. We think we may be all right, but we are not as certain as we would like to be (or we may be quite well, but covet the attention that an indecisive answer solicits). Many older people monitor their physical condition daily and note every evidence of change. They are always on the lookout for the latest prescription drug to allay whatever problem they fear may be approaching.

Overmedicating is a perennial danger, and drugs that were meant to remedy one problem may exacerbate several others. The over-the-counter availability of so many "wonder" drugs leads to indiscriminate use and may leave people in worse condition than they were before taking them. Yet the barrage of advertisements convinces us that there is a quick fix for every discomfort, and, as a result, medicine cabinets get filled with a wide variety of pharmaceuticals. Some senior centers have "Brown Bag Days" when persons are invited to bring all their medications in for a comprehensive evaluation in order to dispose of the those that are outdated and to learn about those that pose a threat when taken together.

In light of all this, it is understandable that a primary topic of conversation for elderly people is the state of one's health. With what sometimes seems to be an almost perverse pleasure, older adults compare symptoms and pains. Many share with one another in great detail all the tests to which they are subjected and take much delight in giving an account of their hospital experience from admission to discharge. Such reporting often comes across as playing the game "Can you top this?"

Predictably, hypochondria may be the result. People can become so preoccupied with their health that there is little else about which to talk. And the more they talk, the higher the anxiety level. We all have acquaintances whom we hesitate to ask the customary, "How are you?" for fear we will receive more information than we care to know. A choice cartoon shows two women walking through a sculpture garden. As they pass a convoluted figure with gaping holes in the torso, one woman exclaims to the other, "Oh, that reminds me of my operation!" Somehow conversations among elderly people keep returning to a comparison of ailments and lead to peer counseling about coping with them. Eventually, one may come to a point where such unrelenting attention to health becomes unhealthy. It is a prevalent danger, not easy for older people to avoid.

Obviously, an obsession with health is likely to generate false fears. At the senior center I frequent, I can always count on seeing the same people returning week after week whenever there is a nurse on duty to give blood pressure checks, ever seeking to allay their anxiety with readings lower than the previous ones. Every new pain may prompt us to ask, "Is this it?" yet we may feel ambivalent about asking our doctor for fear he or she will give the diagnosis we prefer not to hear. We are likely to magnify every minor physical discomfort and to be alarmed by the slightest variation in our vital signs.

Statistics show that the average American life span jumped from forty-nine years in 1900 to an average of seventy-five years in 1990. (Since childbirth is no longer threatening, life expectancy for women has risen from an average of forty-six years at the turn of the century to eighty-two today!) When I was a child, few people lived to be sixty-five, but now over 80 percent of the population does.[3] With this information in mind, we are more likely to be even more concerned about our health as we move toward the age of the average death year. We may tread more slowly and cautiously, believing we are living on borrowed time.

Recently I participated in a public relations project sponsored by our local medical society. Each year the society invites citizens to enroll in what it calls a mini-internship. Its purpose is to afford an opportunity for the laity to gain a better understanding of what a physician's day-to-day life is like. For two consecutive mornings, I donned a white coat and played doctor. I was paired with different specialists to observe their routines and to get an impression of what it would mean to stand in their shoes. One of my companion physicians did nothing but colonoscopies all day long. As I watched her probe the body passageways of dozens of patients whose insides were televised on a large screen adjacent to the examining table, I became increasingly disconcerted and wondered what would be found inside me if I submitted to a similar procedure. My imagination kept those images alive for weeks following. Everyone else's disease became a personal threat; I felt I had comparable symptoms.

Participating in this program revealed how vulnerable I am to the possibility of becoming obsessed with my health. It can happen to anyone. Sometimes the more we know, the more likely we are to worry about things for no rational reason. I even began to understand how Howard Hughes could become so afraid of germs that he became a recluse on the top floor of his luxury hotel in the desert, where he was so reluctant to breathe the air that he always held a tissue to his nose! Here was a tragic case of a man crippled by fear of failing health. Indeed, he mortgaged his life to his dread of dying.

It is not always easy to separate real fears from false fears. At the retirement community where I serve as a board member, a high-voltage power line passes through the property. Some of the residents enjoy working in multiple garden plots located underneath the line. On a recent *Sixty Minutes* television program, the findings of a study indicated that such proximity might pose a serious health hazard by increasing the likelihood of cancer. After the telecast, residents recalled a number of people now deceased who had grown vegetables along the power company right-of-way, and, as they remembered them, their anxiety level began to rise. They insisted on an investigation. The power company quickly counteracted the findings aired on the television program with other studies that indicate there is absolutely no danger to anyone, but the residents were quick to note the vested-interest source of the reassurance (though not equally quick to note the entertainment vested interest of the network to air the story in the most provocative way).

Whether health hazards are real or imagined, older people are socially conditioned to expect decline as they enter their eighties. Mobility problems frequently develop in that decade, and so, as we approach these years, we tend to be more cautious and reticent to take risks. We understand that too much exercise may precipitate death, but we also understand that too little exercise may do so as well. We know the truth of that phrase "Use it or lose it," yet we hesitate to push ourselves too hard. As age advances, we are more likely to define ourselves as the world sees us: as people in need of special care. Even though we may be perfectly capable of continuing the more strenuous activities undertaken in earlier years, we reason it is the better part of wisdom to slow down and not expect as much of ourselves as we once did.

I am a downhill skier, a sport I started in my midforties with my teenage children. Although I will soon be seventy, I still ski, and I greatly enjoy the exhilaration of zooming down the mountain and seeing the splendor of God's creation covered with snow. I have just returned from a week in Utah and seem to be skiing as well, if not better, than I ever did. Of course I tire more quickly, so there is a part of me that questions whether I should be taking this risk. Each successive year I wonder when I will age out, but I try to keep my fear under control and hope I have years ahead of me on the slopes. I still enjoy myself enormously, and it does my ego great good to tag along with the young people, especially now that my grandchildren are also learning to ski. If I thought too much about what *could* happen every time I put on skis, I am sure I would long ago have taken them off and returned to the lodge to sit by the fire instead of standing in line for the chairlift.

I am not advising senior adults to be reckless, but I am suggesting that it may be more foolhardy to worry about what might happen than to assess our ability and do what we want to do despite our age. There is no reason to assume that age brings with it the same liabilities to every older person. Anxiety, fear, and worry can do immeasurable harm if we allow them to get out of bounds.

Another consequence of becoming too health conscious is the likelihood that we will run to the doctor more than we need to go. Obviously, we need to be faithful in scheduling regular medical checkups, but just because we are old does not mean we should see our physician every time we feel an ache or a pain. One of the reasons the cost of health care has risen so steadily is that many people who are basically well have taken a disproportionate share of the caregivers' time. Living in a nation that leads us to believe there is a medical answer for every physical diminution breeds false hopes.

There is a serious shortage of doctors trained in geriatrics in the United States. Although a study in 1980 from the University of California at Los Angeles estimated that at least thirteen thousand doctors who were trained in geriatrics would be needed by 1990, there are now a total of only four thousand who passed a written test and only eight hundred who are fellowship trained. Undergraduate medical students have little instruction in geriatrics, and of the 126 medical schools in the country, only 13 have required courses in geriatrics. Add to these shocking statistics the demographic mismatch, and it is clear that people over sixty-five are not always receiving informed care when they go to their physician. While senior adults make up 13 percent of the population, they use 30 percent of the nation's health-care resources.[4] There is a gap in services of crisis proportion. And so, old people should become more informed consumers and ask in advance if the doctor has had any training in geriatrics. These are the physicians more likely to be committed to improving the quality of life and to see older people in the context of living rather than dying.

Aging is a natural process, and of course there are limits to medical progress. No one can delay death forever by scheduling another appointment with the doctor. It is no secret that the very act of worrying about our physical decline may hasten the day of our dying. The phrase "I'm worried sick" is accurate. It is not uncommon for people to make themselves sick by becoming too obsessive about monitoring their health.

My mother was diagnosed with tuberculosis when I was a child, and she spent a total of two years in a sanatorium and also survived the removal of one diseased lung, but she refused to become an invalid and was more active than most of her peers. I recall her saying on countless occasions, "I'd rather die earlier and enjoy life than become an invalid and live longer." Mother probably should have worried more about her health than she did, but I am convinced that her

refusal to become obsessed with her condition was a significant factor in keeping her alive.

Psychological factors of wellness are probably more important than most of us realize. A strong case can be made for
the belief that we decline in vigor as we age simply because
we have been programmed to do so. We expect it, so we order
our lives accordingly, and, thereby, accelerate it. Innumerable
psychological experiments indicate that the will to live is a
strong factor in ensuring longevity. Sometimes a decision to
move into a retirement community can affect people ad-
versely. They see it as a tacit admission that the time has
come to put on the brakes and prepare for their life journey's
end. But if we anticipate our last years as a time to live
instead of as a time to prepare for death, the chances are that
we will live life more fully.

Christian Scientists have a valid truth in their teaching
that mental attitudes exert considerable power over one's
physical condition. Positive thinking *is* a factor in the way we
feel, and the opposite is also true. If you are constantly
looking for something wrong with yourself, you are more
likely to find it. If you had gotten out of bed feeling fine this
morning, and your spouse had said to you at the breakfast
table, "You don't look well," you probably would have begun
to inventory your condition and consider the possibility that
you might be misreading your sense of well-being. But if you
had dismissed his or her negative diagnosis and subsequently met two friends who said to you in succession, "You
don't seem quite yourself today," before the day was over, you
would likely have declared yourself ill and gone back to bed!
And, to the contrary, if your spouse had said, "You really look
great today," you would likely have emerged from the house
ready to take on the world.

The mind has a powerful influence over our lives. John
Milton, author of *Paradise Lost*, wrote, "The mind is its own
place, and in itself can make a heaven of hell and a hell of
heaven."[5] Recognition of this reality forms the basis of what
we know today as psychosomatic medicine. The mind and
body are intimately related. The Hebrew people understood
this with an anthropology that saw human beings in their

wholeness, unlike the Greeks, whose understanding of our species separated the soul from the body. (Thus, the doctrine of the resurrection of the body comes from the Hebrews, and the idea of the immortality of the soul comes from the Greeks.) The proverb "A merry heart doeth good like a medicine" (Proverbs 17:22) expresses the wisdom of the Jews.

When Norman Cousins, former editor of *The Saturday Review* and one of the most respected men of letters in modern America, suffered a serious illness for which his prognosis was poor, he persuaded his physician to put to the test his belief that laughter might improve his condition. After a steady diet of Laurel and Hardy films, Cousins did indeed get better, as he reports in his book *Anatomy of an Illness*. The book also tells of a visit with Dr. Albert Schweitzer at his African hospital and of Schweitzer's respect for the local witch doctor for understanding that every patient carries his own doctor inside him.[6]

The medical profession uses this discovery by prescribing the placebo, a nonmedical substance that the patient takes under the impression that it is medicine and has curative powers. Because the patient believes this, it often calls forth remarkable improvement in a person's battle against illness. Cousins describes the role of the placebo as follows:

> *Like a celestial chaperon, the placebo leads us through the unchartered passageways of [the] mind. . . . What we see ultimately is that the placebo isn't really necessary and that the mind can carry out its difficult and wondrous missions unprompted by little pills.*[7]

Similarly, when we become obsessed with some health problem, we need to be reassured in order to begin feeling better. The effectiveness of the reassurance is in large measure determined by the confidence we have in its source, and, for most people, this means a trusted physician. I recall the second day of my mini-internship when I was paired with a pediatrician. We saw scores of crying children, but, in most cases, the main treatment the doctor offered was to the mothers who needed to be told authoritatively that nothing was seriously wrong with their babies. He acknowledged to me afterward that a major part of his practice consisted of counseling parents who were without experience in what to expect in child rearing.

Recently I went through a three-month period of insomnia. It was horrendous. Night after night I had trouble going to sleep. I tried everything, and nothing seemed to make much difference. I took more exercise. I read during the night. I listened to soothing music. Nothing worked. I became a walking zombie. Then I began taking over-the-counter sleeping pills, which gave me partial relief. But this too became problematic, for I worried about becoming addicted to the medication.

Finally, I made an appointment at the hospital with a sleep specialist. I was desperate, but many of my peers said, "Welcome to the club; this is the way it is when you get older. You don't require as much sleep as you once did." But I was unwilling to accept my condition as normative and looked forward to a professional opinion. I was convinced that something was seriously wrong, and the less I slept, the more worried I became. The physician was a godsend. She spent two leisurely hours with me and asked every predictable question and many more. "Are you under stress?" she asked. Of course I was under stress! I was not sleeping, and the less I slept, the more stressed-out I felt. The outcome was strong reassurance from the physician but no medication. She told me that I was probably suffering from some fluke that had nothing to do with either my aging or my physical condition. She believed my insomnia would diminish if I gradually ceased taking the sleeping pills. She was right. Within a month, I was sleeping eight hours per night on my very own! As I look back upon this protracted agonizing experience, I am sure I helped create the crisis by my obsession, which I also later helped cure.

I must acknowledge that my religion offered some help too, but not to the extent I had wanted. I tried to use the long night watches to meditate and pray, but, although there was no miracle, these expressions of faith did have a steadying influence. I gained a new appreciation of several of the Psalms in which the psalmist writes of waiting anxiously through the night for the coming of the morning. I also identified with Job's complaining to God because he was suffering for reasons he could not understand.

I do not want to exaggerate the power of the mind over the body. Clearly there are many diseases and physical conditions that are not amenable to change no matter what one's attitude may be. Belief may influence biology, but it is surely false to imply that people should feel responsible for the ills that beset them. As a pastor, I quickly learned how harmful it is to give to sick people the impression that they are suffering because they do not have sufficient faith to get well. That is the way Deepak Chopra's widely read new book, *Ageless Body, Timeless Mind*, affected me.[8] He makes incredible claims about halting the aging process by mental awareness of the physiology and psychological processes that keep us alive. He has taken a half-truth and made it the whole truth. (Or perhaps it is more charitable to say that he has exaggerated in the direction of truth.) It seems irresponsible to suggest that we have within ourselves unlimited potential for extending our life span. It is simply not true that if you set your mind to remain young you can remain youthful indefinitely. Such counsel sounds very much like the prophet telling the people what they want to hear. Already over one million copies are in circulation, claiming the amazing possibility of an ageless body and a timeless mind.

Fortunately, most of us gradually ease into old age. It is seldom a matter of waking up one morning and suddenly realizing we are old. As we enter old age, we can negotiate what is within the realm of the possible and what our waning strength will no longer permit. But we may become so anxious about our physical well-being that we will find ourselves pursuing health for health's sake only. It is important to understand that good health should never be an end in itself. Life is meant to be lived for the sake of living and not for the sake of avoiding death. The critical question is What do I want to do with the life my good health gives me? not simply How do I perpetuate the health that I have?

We have an almost insatiable desire to live longer and longer, but we are beginning to accept the judgment that there comes a time when living just for the sake of living is not desirable. We recognize that the length of life can be far from a blessing unless it is accompanied by quality of life. When Jesus said, "I have come that they may have life, and that they may have it more abundantly" (John 10:10, NKJV), he was not talking about increasing our age span but increasing the quality of the life we have. He was not promising more years to our lives but more life to our years.

For most of us, the phrase "quality of life" suggests the possession of a clear mind and at least tolerable health. A speaker at one of our senior-center luncheons asked those present, "How many of you would like to live to be one hundred?" All hesitated to raise their hands. It was obvious that no one wanted to live that long without first being assured that he or she would not simply be vegetating. Keeping alive just to remain alive is not enough. Indeed the pursuit of health is similar to the pursuit of happiness. You seldom achieve it if it is your sole goal in life. More often it comes as the by-product of a fully engaged lifestyle.

Do you recall the story about the proverbial Texas millionaire who had worked hard all of his life to be rich? He had dreamed of making enough money to buy expensive cars, and near the end of his life, he had at last amassed a large enough fortune to purchase his long-coveted Cadillac. But on that very day, he died! His family members decided that nothing would please their deceased loved one more than to bury him in his new automobile, and that is exactly what they did. As they lowered the fancy car and driver into the enormous grave, a grave digger leaning on a shovel nearby exclaimed, "Man, that's what I call really living!" Surely really living involves something more than merely the appearance of being alive!

Waning health cannot be forestalled forever. Aging is a part of the normal life cycle. The sooner we make peace with this fact, the more peaceful and less obsessive about health we are likely to be. Although medical science has made great strides forward, there is always a ragged edge to life beyond which all the king's men cannot put us together again. Physicians can delay decline and death only for a time, never permanently.

There is a further important consideration that should not be overlooked as we enter the last years of life. You do not need perfect health to be productive, nor even to be happy. Look around you. There are people of all ages who have learned how to live with disabilities. Their example should be a source of considerable encouragement to those who suffer some physical diminishment late in life. Yes, it is possible to cope with crippling handicaps without being obsessed with your health. I was in a store recently and overheard a conversation between the clerk and an old man who was obviously a frequent customer. The clerk asked, "How are you feeling today?" The gentleman replied with a smile, "I'm aching all over, but that means I'm working."

A recent teleplay on *American Playhouse* titled "Home" depicted a story of a courageous, determined older woman who lived in a condominium cluster in Florida, in a unit alone. Her three grown daughters lived in cities far away. The woman fell and suffered a serious break of her hip, and of course all of the children flew in to respond to the crisis. Almost immediately, they began to set in motion a plan to move her from the hospital into a nursing home and to put her condo up for sale. But their mother would have none of it. She was adamant in her intent to return to where she had lived and was not about to surrender her independence, despite what had happened. Reluctantly, her daughters relented and allowed her to return to the condominium. Within days, they were amazed to see their mother walk across the entire length of the living room without assistance. It was as if her determination had demanded that her hip obey her will. The woman was convinced that, though her mobility would be slower and that she would have to be more cautious in the future, she could nevertheless continue her life where she had lived before.

Happiness is possible even when health is fragile and waning. The restrictions imposed by impairments in one area can be lessened by compensation in another. Attention to a larger agenda of interests than our physical well-being is probably more healthy in the long run than becoming so obsessed with health care that we are unable to care about anything else. Not every illness can be overcome, but disabilities need not destroy the quality of our lives. Dr. Mark Williams of the University of North Carolina School of Medicine says that the medical charts of older patients often fail to note the things he needs to know, those unique, identifying things that make us the individuals we are. He approaches every physical problem with an assessment of the patient's unique abilities, including strengths and limitations.

My preaching professor at Yale Divinity School insisted that students learn how to preach from a manuscript. He felt it was good discipline to write out a sermon in full and have the complete text before you at the time of the sermon's delivery. He warned, however, that one should never succumb to the danger of appearing overly dependent upon the manuscript, and advised, "The only effective way to use a manuscript is to treat it with contempt; never hold onto it as if for dear life." It occurs to me that this same advice applies to the way we monitor our health. If we try to hold on to it as if for dear life, our life performance will inevitably suffer. But if we cease worrying about our health and have the courage to embrace life with confidence, we will likely be amazed by our ability to do things we might otherwise never attempt or think possible.

It is a good thing to have good health, but an obsession with health is unhealthy.

Chapter 7

Achieving Personal Integration

Biographers know that it is difficult to accurately assess anyone's life until you see it from the perspective of his or her old age, and frequently, not until after that person's death. Traits of one's early age become more pronounced at midlife and usually stand out with predictable consistency as one grows old. Behavioral patterns are also more easily detected by looking back over the years to observe how someone responded to similar situations from one stage of life to another. Indeed, many older adults acknowledge that one of their discoveries in the aging process is that the older we get, the better we understand ourselves. Perhaps this is the beginning of wisdom.

This may be why older adults often undertake writing their memoirs or keep journals. There seems to be a need to review our personal history and to achieve a sense of closure about what we have done with our lives before our years end. It is almost as if we want to set the record straight by recording and reconciling all of the events of our past. We want to weave the various threads together into a finished tapestry. (This may also be why we like to talk about the past. It is easier than writing about it and may fill some of the same purposes and needs.)

I can understand this impulse. Soon after my retirement I wrote an account of my lifelong struggle with racism in our society.[1] I grew up in a segregated South Carolina town, and I was continually involved in civil rights issues during my North Carolina pastorates. As I reflected upon my life story, racism emerged as the central theme of both my formative years and my professional career. Writing the retrospective enabled me to bring my life into focus and to see clearly aspects of my personality that I had never previously acknowledged.

Looking back over the years and noting the way I responded to those crucial events was a therapeutic experience. It helped me to understand better who I am. I could see how in the midst of continuing change I was constantly becoming more like myself. As a consequence, I felt more comfortable with myself and realized for the first time why I had acted the way I did in certain situations long since past.

Something similar to this probably happens to most older people. Aging stimulates us to think about our past, and this helps us not only to get a more accurate reading about ourselves but also motivates us to new levels of authenticity, integrity, and personal integration. We want to approach the end of our life feeling good about where we have been and what we have done. To arrive at such a resolution may not be possible for everyone, but for those who make the effort, it is surely rewarding.

Almost inevitably we become involved in such a process as we begin sorting out our memories. I have just completed reading again the letters my mother wrote to me while I was away in college. It was an eye-opening experience, for at this late stage of my life I can more readily identify with her perception of me as a young boy far away from home. I read between the lines revelations about myself that I never picked up when I received her correspondence more than a half century ago.

Whenever we probe our past, some of the memories that surface can be so painful that we may be tempted to suppress them, but there is strong professional opinion that, unless we are willing to look at them, they are likely to haunt us. Even late in life many such memories can be dealt with effectively and finally by seeking forgiveness, making amends, offering restitution or by confessing things to ourselves that we have been loath to admit before. By so doing, we can remove festering resentment from situations that remain unresolved. Holding on to hatred or grudges against anyone is more harmful to ourselves in the long run than to the person to whom it is directed. Just as the passing of the years takes its toll on us physically, so does repressed anger or guilt accelerate aging by stifling our spirit. We are far better off when we resist keeping alive painful experiences from yesterday and reach out with a reconciling overture toward anyone whose recall to our memory affects us negatively. We should close the books on old debts and cease opening old wounds. We would do well to emulate the posture of the apostle Paul, who wrote:

> *The one thing I do, however, is to forget what is behind me and do my best to reach what is ahead. So I run straight toward the goal in order to win the prize, which is God's call through Christ Jesus to the life above. All of us who are spiritually mature should have this same attitude (Philippians 3:13-15, GNB).*

Edward Albee's dazzling new play, *Three Tall Women*, is about memories. The central character is a ninety-two-year-old matriarch. The plot develops as if someone had pushed the replay button on her life, for she floats in and out of senility to look at pivotal experiences from her past. One electrifying scene recounts a breakup with her son decades before when she learned he was homosexual. As that part of her life is recalled, the son appears by her bed and stands there saying nothing, but, with mute devotion, he holds her hand and strokes her forehead. The scene suggests that at last some sort of resolution of a long-term alienation has finally occurred.

Some older people settle for reminiscing instead of creating new memories. Although reminiscing is one of the pleasures of advanced age, we must be careful lest its excess cause us to retreat from the present. In the recent best-selling book *Having Our Say*, two one-hundred-year-old black sisters share their wit and wisdom and wonderful memories. Although they were reared in the South at a time when the region was rigidly prejudiced, they are able to recall positive experiences, having managed their memories well and left behind all bitterness about what they endured there. Even as centenarians, they are able to live in the present and continue to cherish what each day brings.[2]

Memories often surface when we least expect them. An event in the present may suddenly call to mind a similar situation long ago. Such uninvited recollections can call forth emotional responses comparable to what we felt when the incidents first occurred. Elise Maclay, in her poem "Nostalgia," puts it this way:

> . . . *Nostalgia*
> *Is a two-edged sword,*
> *The joy of remembering*
> *Is as sharp as the pain,*
> *Comes when I least expect it,*
> *Cuts me to ribbons.*
> *Strange, when the young speak of aging,*
> *They use words like mellow.*
> *They imagine memory to be a soft amber glow,*
> *When, in reality, You and I know,*
> *It is more like a laser beam.*[3]

A major interest in divinity schools today is evaluating the retrospectives of one's life pilgrimage. It forms the basis for what is called story theology. The thesis is that in every life there is evidence of divine activity. I believe it is true that most older people can detect God's involvement in their personal history if they are willing to look at their lives from a theological perspective. Life has brought to us many good things beyond our own choosing that might properly be recognized as gifts of God's creation. And in every life there are those unplanned opportunities that open up for us or those fortuitous encounters that influence our life direction. All such incidents beyond our arranging can be explained as the work of God's providence. Then there are those tragic and hurtful things we suffer in life from which some good mysteriously emerges. This is what people of faith call God's redemptive activity, bringing something good out of something bad. Happy are those who can detect God's hand in their life story, who can winnow their memories. Happy are those who can look back over many years and realize they have been blessed by the promise of the psalmist that "goodness and mercy shall follow me all the days of my life. . . ." (Psalm 23:6).

Aging brings us to life's extremity, and extremities have a way of revealing our mettle and stripping away all societal conditionings and cosmetic masks. Just as the prodigal son found himself in a situation where he was totally helpless and "came to himself" (Luke 15:17), so do those in the far country of aging often find themselves pushed to the limit. We then have an opportunity to become more authentically who we are with a depth of integrity seldom realized at any early age. We come to ourselves.

It is one thing to know ourselves. It is something else to accept ourselves. Both are prerequisites to experiencing a genuine sense of personal integration.

All of us would like to look back over our lives and feel good about the route we have chosen, the decisions we have made, and the way we have responded to the challenges and opportunities that came our way. Yet there is an all-too-common temptation to ponder what might have happened if we had taken a different fork in the road or married another person or prepared for some other vocation. Dwelling upon what might have been rather than accepting what actually occurred can have an adverse effect upon our final years.

We may also compromise our limited future if we refuse to come to terms with aspects of our character or personality that we have tried to conceal. For example, we may find it necessary to confess that ulterior motives account for more of our altruism than we prefer to admit. (I have had to acknowledge that my many volunteer involvements are essential for the sake of my self-esteem. I have a great need to feel needed.) Or we may look back over our lives and see a recurring pattern of blame shifting. All of us are capable of creating carefully crafted rationalizations to sustain our self-image, offering explanations that would be difficult to defend convincingly.

Seeing our true selves may also require a more honest admission of our own particular combination of masculine and feminine characteristics. In *Fountain of Age* Betty Friedan makes a strong case for her judgment that, as people age, women become more like men and men become more like women. She sees women becoming more aggressive with age and men becoming more gentle, as if we were changing sex roles. It is generally understood that each of us represents a blending of both gender characteristics from the time of our birth, but cultural pressure usually succeeds in defining our behavior more rigidly toward one sex or the other. Perhaps a more accurate interpretation of the statement that God "created them male and female" (Genesis 1:27, GNB) is that God made each individual with a combination of both sexes. When we are old it may be easier to acknowledge and hold in balance a part of ourselves that might have seemed unacceptable when we were young. We are less threatened by honest revelations about ourselves in our last years than when we were pressured by our teenage peers to conform to sexual stereotypes.

It would be hard to review our lives and conclude that we had wasted our years and that our efforts have added up to little or nothing. It would also be difficult for persons who are prone to perfectionism to believe they have failed to measure up to their full potential and thus assess their accomplishments as unacceptable. It would be painful to come to life's end and feel the kind of desperation so vividly described by Shakespeare as Macbeth judges himself to have violated both his own and society's standards:

My way of life
Is fall'n into the sear, the yellow leaf,
And that which should accompany old age,
As honor, love, obedience, troops of friends,
I must not look to have.[4]

But, whatever the case, there is a way to come to the last chapter in one's life and say, "It is well, it is well, with my soul." The central affirmation of the Christian faith is that anyone can be made acceptable by accepting God's gracious outreach to each of us in Christ. We do not warrant this acceptance either on the basis of our achievements or our failures but solely on the basis of our acknowledgment of our need. Self-acceptance then becomes possible not because of anything we have done or can do but because of what God has done and continues to do.

Nothing short of a sense of ultimate acceptance will suffice if we hope to complete our last years with a sense of inward peace. The assurance of God's acceptance liberates us from the need to be preoccupied with the past, for, in the final analysis, the record of our previous behavior is irrelevant in the awareness of God's forgiveness and love. The only sure way to feel good about ourselves is to understand that we are embraced by One who always stands ready to renew us and to offer another opportunity to become what God intended us to be.

Theologian Paul Tillich has written extensively about our ability to accept ourselves, and these are his words:

> *Man can love himself in terms of self-acceptance only if he is certain that he is accepted. Otherwise his self-acceptance is self-complacency and arbitrariness. Only in the light and in the power of love from above can he love himself.*[5]

The only thing required is that we divest ourselves of pretense and power and accept our acceptance, trusting our lives to God just as we are "without one plea." Unfortunately, some people find this an exceedingly difficult thing to do, for it means standing totally exposed and defenseless in the presence of God.

One telling indication of our having accepted ourselves is that we cease taking ourselves too seriously. We no longer need to prove ourselves, so we can lay to rest all illusory ambitions. We should now be secure enough to laugh at ourselves and not feel it necessary to justify ourselves for anything we have done. A saving grace at any age is a sense of humor, and especially as we grow older.

Self-knowledge and self-acceptance are prerequisites for achieving a sense of personal integration, and they pave the way for yet another desirable goal: self-transcendence. This brings us to the essence of spirituality, going beyond the self and understanding that our hope for the future can no longer be centered in our own ego but lies in the promise of our finitude being linked with the Infinite. "Letting go to let God" is a religious principle appropriate to any age, but elderly people must learn to do this with diminishing reservation and resistance. Letting go is a courageous act of faith, for it involves coming to a new place and seeing life from a new perspective. We not only accept the contingency of our existence and perceive how fragile life is, we also acknowledge an impinging Presence from beyond who touches our lives with reassurance and comforts us in the awareness of our ultimate security. It is tantamount to acknowledging our limitations and mortality. Instead of relying on our self-sufficiency, we risk trusting our lives to a spiritual reality that we can experience but never fully prove.

Because our culture puts such a high premium on competence, competition, and the ability to control, it can be a wrenching experience to abdicate the driver's seat and take seriously the realization that we are not in charge of everything. All past activities that gave us a sense of power and fostered the illusion of our indispensable importance tend to nurture an oversized ego. Aging has a way of puncturing this balloon and making it quite clear that if the future is centered in ourselves alone, we can only despair.

I have a retired friend who never misses an opportunity to tell me about all of his achievements, the money he has made, and the important people he knows. For him it is still necessary to see himself as a power broker and as one who can pull whatever strings are needed to accomplish incredible deals. He has an enormous ego, and, despite declining health, he has not yet faced up to the approaching day when he will likely be helpless. Most of us share such deception. Though we know intellectually that we may soon be in no condition to call the shots about anything, we prefer to contemplate that next week, but not now.

Other older people settle for another game plan to perpetuate their egocentrism. After they surrender whatever power roles they once played in the world, they cleverly manipulate those around them to feed an ego that refuses to relinquish former attention. Friends and family can never do enough for them. They repeatedly remind everyone of ways they can express their love and allegiance. They become masters in the art of making people feel guilty if there is any hint of anyone's waning adulation or lapse of attentiveness. (This becomes even more effective if they have a debilitating physical condition!) These aging matriarchs or patriarchs feel that their opinion about anything should be respected and revered by all their acquaintances, and anyone who dares to disagree soon learns that he or she is out of favor. Such behavior should be recognized for what it is—pure self-centeredness—and self-centeredness is not pretty at any age. The only way to help a person who relates to us in this way is to refuse to play the game.

There are other people who avoid the pitfalls thus far described and manage to gracefully surrender their power roles for a lifestyle that seldom puts themselves out front. On occasion their approach to the world appears almost ethereal, for their primary focus is the well-being of others. The mainspring of their lives seems to be an outpouring of gratitude, expressed by generosity and good works directed toward their family, their friends, people in poverty, or those caught in other life crises. They never seek the limelight or crave credit for anything they do. Their sole reward is in the joy of doing it. Like a cup that is full and "runneth over," their lives brim with a love that is readily offered to anyone. At times their lives seem almost transparent for they never draw attention to themselves. Their lives are living illustrations of what Jesus asked of all of us: "Let your light so shine before men, that they may see your good works and glorify your Father in heaven" (Matthew 5:16, NKJV). Such individuals are moving toward self-transcendence and are aware of Another who is in control; they know it is God who has made us and not we ourselves.

There is something wonderfully liberating when we reach the point of understanding that not everything depends on us and that, after all, we are only human, finite creatures. That truth alone could be somewhat unsettling were it not for one's faith in an almighty God who holds "the whole world in His hands." You and I are dependent beings, and human life is exceedingly fragile. Yet persons of faith can rest in the thought that the One to whom we belong knows the number of even the hairs on our heads and loves each one of us more than a mother loves her only child. These reassurances learned early in life take on a new level of meaning as we edge toward possible infirmity and certain infinity.

Self-transcendence is also relevant to the way we view our bodies. As we grow older, we know that eventually we can expect physical decline and debilitation. Gradually, many bodily functions that healthy people take for granted begin to fail. The activity of our lives slows down, and we define our existence more and more in terms of how well we feel instead of what we can do. Being takes precedence over doing.

When diseases associated with the aging process bring with them severe handicaps and excruciating pain, each day becomes an ongoing contest between the claims of the physical and the comfort of the spiritual. This struggle can precipitate the emergence of unforeseen inner strength and become a catalyst for personal transformation. Like the apostle Paul, who suffered from an unnamed "thorn in the flesh," we discover that divine power often manifests itself in weakness and that even in a time of distress we are able to look beyond our condition to glorify God. As Paul himself said, "We who have this spiritual treasure are like common clay pots, in order to show that the supreme power belongs to God, not to us" (2 Corinthians 4:7, GNB).

The reality of the spiritual may intensify as the physical part of us wanes and weakens. This has been the experience of people of faith down through the centuries, and testimony to this effect appears in the literature of the saints throughout the history of the church. Typical of such accounts is a volume from 150 years ago titled *Happy Talk Towards the End of Life*, from which the following statement is quoted:

> *Is your eyesight dimmer? Then the world is seen by you in cathedral light. Is your hearing duller? Then it is just as though you were always where loud voices and footsteps ought not to be heard. . . . Yes, for twilight and silence . . . old age makes us like daily dwellers in the house of the Lord.*[6]

When John Quincy Adams was eighty years old, he was asked by a friend, "How is Mr. Adams today?" The former president is reported to have replied, "He is quite well, thank you, but the house in which he lives is becoming a little dilapidated; in fact, almost uninhabitable. I think John Adams will have to move out before long. But he, himself, is well, thank you, quite well."

Our destiny is to transcend the physical altogether, for we are primarily spiritual beings, and this transition begins in the here and now. The apostle Paul states this in his Corinthians correspondence, where he writes about our physical decline being offset by a daily spiritual renewal (2 Corinthians 4:16). Eventually we slough off the physical altogether, and, as the psalmist puts it, we "fly away" (Psalm 90:10).

When our physical body begins to seem more like a burden than a blessing, we may experience a spiritual uplift if we can see our existence in a larger context by affirming our connectedness to all of God's creation. Age seems to bring with it an expanding awareness of the mystery of the world and a greater sense of wonder about the life cycle, our coming and our going. It is a time when we are more likely to marvel at nature and stand and stare as we contemplate the intricacy and inexplicableness of it all. We begin to see ourselves less as a separate being and more as a part God's whole creation. Our sense of personal integration expands to embrace the universe. And it embraces us too.

American transcendentalist Margaret Fuller, who was a pioneer feminist and literary editor of the *New York Tribune*, was a friend of Ralph Waldo Emerson. One day she announced to the world in her newspaper that she had decided to accept the universe, to which Emerson replied, "By Gad! She'd better!" When we are in the prime of life, it is tempting to see ourselves as the center around which the universe revolves, but aging has a way of reversing that audacity and forcing us to feel humbled before it all.

You may recall an earlier comment about the book *The Courage to Grow Old*, a collection of essays written by celebrities about aging. Although there is precious little reference made by any of them to traditional religion, nearly all of them speak of their heightened sensitivity to nature and the mystery of the natural world. Indeed, some of their statements read like religious mysticism, as if nature itself summons us to higher levels of consciousness, transcending our physical limitations. The transition to this new awareness is captured by the poet Archibald MacLeish as he contrasts the way he viewed God's creation early and later in life:

At twenty, stooping round about,
I thought the world a miserable place,
Truth a trick, faith in doubt,
Little beauty, less grace.

Now at sixty what I see,
Although the world is worse by far,
Stops my heart in ecstasy.
God, the wonders that there are![7]

This awe of the universe and heightened sense of the mystery of life often leads older people to be more open and questioning about traditional religion and even to become agnostic. Indeed, people who in their earlier years may have been quite conservative and orthodox in their faith may become less certain that they have the whole truth as they grow older. This change does not so much indicate a doubting of religious faith as it represents a judgment that it is presumptuous for anyone to boast of adequately defining and describing divinity. People who may once have been dogmatic in assuming their beliefs to be superior those of others often become more mellow and ready to respect the convictions of people who do not recite the same creed.

Dag Hammarskjöld, who was a man of great personal faith, once said, "God does not die on the day we cease to believe in a personal deity, but we die on the day when our lives cease to be illumined by the steady radiance, renewed daily, of a wonder, the source of which is beyond all reason."[8] This sentiment speaks for countless older adults who experience a deepening spirituality late in life but who think it cannot be contained within what they judge to be the narrow boundaries of traditional creeds. (Yet a popular stereotype of older people is that they are conservative and unbending in their beliefs.)

For many elderly people, every day is a miracle, and "the heavens declare the glory of God" (Psalm 19:1). There seems a willingness not only to look beyond one's ego to see oneself as a part of God's creation but a desire to join with all the music of the spheres in celebrating our place in the unfathomable unity. The novelist Ellen Glasgow speaks for many spiritually sensitive senior adults in saying:

> *When I think of dying . . . it is not of dying as a cold negation, but as a warm and friendly welcome to the universe, the Being beyond and above consciousness, or any vestige of. . . . All I know is that I look at death as the other side of life. . . . In my death, as my life, I am still seeking God.*

Self-transcendence finds further expression in the ability of older people to look beyond their own time in history to the future. It is not unusual to hear them say, "I hope to live to see . . .," but whether or not they do, many elderly individuals deed the assets of their estates to causes that make the world a better place for those who will inhabit the earth long after they are gone. Like Moses, who looked out over the Promised Land but was not permitted to enter it, we can project ourselves far beyond our years to make a difference in someone else's tomorrow. This is also a form of self-transcendence.

We begin life as totally dependent beings, and we may end life as totally dependent beings. Having moved through the in-between stages of independence and interdependence, it is not easy to give up self-reliance to surrender ourselves once again to complete dependence on others. We can identify with that poignant plea of the psalmist, "Cast me not off in the time of old age" (Psalm 71:9). Old people who are surrounded by caring family members, caregivers, and supportive friends are fortunate, but even more fortunate are those who learn how to rely on the grace of God.

Grace is a theological word that can be defined simply as the unmerited extra in life that comes to us over and beyond our ability to call it forth. It is that plus factor that meets us in times of extremity and enables us to keep going. Grace sees us through situations we thought we could never survive.

The nature of grace is suggested by that homespun story about the Yankee who was traveling through the South and stopped at a small-town corner cafe for breakfast. He ordered his usual eggs, bacon, and toast, but when his food arrived, there were grits on his plate, something he had never been served before. "Waitress!" he protested, "I didn't order these," to which she warmly replied, "You don't have to order them, mister, they just come." Grace is like that. It just comes, and the proper response is gratitude.

Generally speaking, older adults find it easy to believe in grace. As we wind down from our more strenuous years, we gradually concede the necessity of admitting our weakened condition and our need to lean on the goodness of God and the graciousness of others to sustain us. It is often hard to be on the receiving end if we have been accustomed to the role of one who gives, but grace enables us to complete this role reversal. Gradually we learn to rely on the promise that God's mercy is "new every morning" (Lamentations 3:23). We find comfort in the assurance that God's "grace is sufficient" for all of life's contingencies and also experience the paradoxical truth that God's "strength is made perfect in weakness" (2 Corinthians 12:9).

As we review our life stories in old age, most of us realize in retrospect that we have faced things we never thought we could have faced, such as the discovery of breast cancer at age forty. We have coped in crises where we never thought we could, such as in saying goodbye to our son when he was drafted to go to Vietnam. We have endured beyond our ability to endure, such as in caring for our aging parents who lived to be ninety-five. We not only have persevered but have prevailed. And how did we do it? Surely it was possible because of the grace of God. Remembrance of such occasions enables us to believe that we will not be forsaken as once again we commence a difficult period, requiring more faith than we feel we possess. We are comforted by that confident line from the hymn: "So long thy power hast blessed us; sure it still will lead me on."

Robert Browning's couplet from Rabbi ben Ezra, "Grow old along with me! The best is yet to be," is considered by some people to be a Pollyanna assessment of old age. Unfortunately, the two lines are usually quoted without the remaining part that follows. In the continuation of the poem, Browning explains why he makes this claim. He believed the last of life is best because that is when we consummate our lifelong relationship with our Creator. He understood old age to be a time of total self-surrender to God's creative finishing touch. And this is what he wrote:

> *But I need, now as then,*
> *Thee, God, who moldest men; . . .*
> *So, take and use Thy work;*
> *Amend what flaws may lurk,*
> *What strain o' the stuff,*
> *What warpings past the aim!*
> *My times be in Thy hand!*
> *Perfect the cup as planned!*[9]

Chapter 8

Paying Attention to the Exit Signs

Woody Allen once said, "I don't mind dying; I just don't want to be there when it happens." Most people share his ambivalence about death—whatever their age.

Even from early childhood, many of us were taught by rote that death is always an imminent possibility by praying this same prayer night after night at bedtime:

If I should die before I wake,
I pray thee, Lord, my soul to take.

Psychiatrists judge this to be an inappropriate petition for the very young because it may nurture a fear of death before they are able to understand it. But children are not the only ones who find it difficult to deal with death. We all do. In the vibrant years of youth, death seems so far away that the promise of the Resurrection may not sound like good news. And in the middle years, when the sand in the hour glass shifts more swiftly, we try to ignore death and assume it happens to other people but not to us.

The leading character in the novel *The Sheltering Sky* notes that, though death is always on the way, "the fact that you don't know when it will arrive seems to take away from the finiteness of life. It's that terrible precision that we hate so much. But because we don't know, we get to think of life as an inexhaustible well."[1] In Tolstoy's story, "The Death of Ivan Illyich," a dying man suddenly realizes what is happening. A chill comes over him, and he suffers acute anxiety, for he had somehow thought it would be impossible for death to overtake him. Ivan remembers his class in logic where he learned the syllogism:

Caius is a man.
All men are mortal.

Therefore, Caius is mortal.[2]

This reasoning had seemed correct when applied to Caius, but Ivan protested that he was not Caius, not an abstract person but a unique, irreplaceable human being. Surely he was an exception!

Who of us has not felt that way? So long as we continue saying, *"If* I should die . . .," death is easier to contemplate, for this seems to suggest that we might somehow avoid it. But as we age, we realize this is misleading and that the word *if* must be replaced with the word *when*. Death is down the road for each of us, and we are moving inexorably toward it. As one older person put it, "I feel like I am on an escalator moving down."

Recently I stopped at the desk of the YMCA to inquire about the status of my membership. I had lost my membership card and thought it was about time to have it renewed. The young woman on duty looked in vain for a record of my account. Then she turned to me and asked, "Mr. Seymour, are you sure you're not expired?" I could not conceal my amusement and replied flippantly, "No, I think I am very much alive!" But the conversation left me with somber thoughts. I was reminded of my mortality and my approaching death, and I realized that her use of the word "expired" was very much in line with biblical teaching, for Genesis describes how God created Adam by breathing into him the breath of life.

As we advance in age, many acquaintances precede us in death. We read obituary columns more faithfully. When we find the name of someone we know, especially one of our peers, we experience some degree of shock, for we understand our time of departure is nearing. We see ourselves standing in line, descending on that escalator, and we begin to be more attentive to the exit signs.

Fortunately, we are living in an era when death is no longer a taboo topic and can be discussed more openly. American society once treated the subject almost as if it were pornography. Everyone thought about death but considered it offensive to talk about it. We owe a considerable debt of gratitude to Dr. Elisabeth Kübler-Ross for helping to change this. Her widely read book *On Death and Dying* led to a greater willingness by both professionals and the public at large to address the topic more openly. Also, Evelyn Waugh's satirical novel *The Loved One* had an indirect influence. Waugh lampoons the absurd lengths to which morticians go to deny the reality of death. Further significant impact in challenging prevalent funeral practices was made by Jessica Mitford's *American Way of Death*, published in the early seventies.

This new openness makes it easier for physicians, patients, and their families to face more forthrightly those difficult decisions that must be made when death occurs or someone is suffering from a terminal disease. Not long ago it was generally considered unkind to tell the truth to a dying patient. Caregivers reasoned that the dying person should not be deprived of hope, but, as a consequence, people were denied the use of their last days in ways as such sobering knowledge might have prompted. Or worse, patients who knew full well that death was approaching refused to "let on" and played the cruel game of "Let's pretend everything is going to be OK" in order to "protect" their family and friends. Today it is commonplace to keep patients fully informed about their condition, and the people dying are thus able to have a say in what kind of treatment they receive and when it is best to cease battling the inevitable.

Just before Senator Jacob Javits died, he wrote an article for *The New York Times* titled "Life, Death, and Human Dignity." In it he said:

> *I may be terminally ill. I therefore face, in an intimate and personal way, the issue of my right to die. I am happy for those who are not ill, but they are terminal too and they should think about this question as it relates to themselves and those they love* . . .[3]

Javits was advocating that old people give prior thought both to *when* they want to die and *how* they want to die. These considerations are new to this generation because of the major changes that have occurred in modern medicine and technology during our lifetime.

Richard Lamm, the former governor of Colorado, stirred up quite a public flap several years ago when the press

reported that he had said elderly people "have a duty to die."
Subsequently, it was clear that the governor had been quoted
out of context. Nevertheless, he voiced a legitimate concern
about something that has become a pressing issue for people
of advanced age. Should we insist on continuing our lives with
costly survival technology when it is obvious that life is
essentially over? A whole new agenda of ethical problems has
arisen because of the economics of modern medicine. How
much longer can we justify spending hundreds of thousands
of dollars on the continuing care of critically ill patients who
have no vestige of quality of life left and no hope of improving?
According to Dr. Mark Williams, surveys show that the average person in America may pay 70 percent of all he or she
ever spends for health care in the last year of life! (This
statistic is not valid for people over age eighty.)

The Bible states that there is "a time to be born and a time
to die" (Ecclesiastes 3:2), but today the time to die is not as
easily determined as it once was. Indeed, the approach of
death has become increasingly problematic now that contemporary medical practice has found ways to keep people
breathing indefinitely. We are so blessed by life extension
that it is common for old people to live far beyond the biblical
limit of "three-score years and ten." We are living longer and
enjoying it more. But, as Governor Lamm reminded his
audience, to look for immortality through medical miracles
is as useless as attempting to glue the leaves back on the trees
when winter comes.

What we once understood as natural death is not as clear
as it once was. For example, earlier generations considered
it natural for people to die prematurely of pneumonia or
tuberculosis, but now that these diseases can be effectively
treated, we would not think it natural for young people to die
from them. Today, a more general understanding of what
constitutes natural death is the withholding of prolonged
medical intervention when there is no hope for a cure. But
there is no consensus, and, as a result, the debate continues
about how much should be done for those who are critically
ill beyond all hope of recovery.

Dr. Daniel Callahan, director of the Institute of Society,

Ethics, and Life Science, offers what he calls a stipulative definition of natural death, the kind of death most people would probably choose if they could. Natural death, he says, is that point in the life span when: (a) one's life work has been accomplished; (b) one's moral obligations to those for whom one has responsibility have been discharged; (c) one's death will not seem an offense to sensibility or cause others to despair at human existence; and (d) one's process of dying is not marked by unbearable and degrading pain.[4]

This last condition warrants our most careful advance attention, for, ironically, at a time when old age is less frightening and even a stage of life to which we may look forward, the prospect of a long and lingering death is more fearsome than ever before. We are losing our right to die when it is time to die. We are also forfeiting the way we want to die.

I recall so vividly my grandfather's death. He died at home of natural causes. He was in his own bed and surrounded by family. I was a young teen at the time, and I shall never forget those solemn last hours as we said goodbye to him. We all understood that the time had come for him to go, and my grandfather made the transition aware of strong ties of love that sustained him. Now 80 percent of elderly people commonly die behind white curtains in a hospital among strangers. The prospect is disturbing, almost inhumane in its lack of sensitivity to the spiritual and emotional well-being of the person whose life is slipping away.

Listen further to Governor Lamm:

> When we start using machines which don't cure or heal—which don't prolong life but extend dying, when we use them trying in vain to stop the irreversible, often at great pain to the patient, then we have abdicated not only our role as moral men and women, but our very humanness. We are making human sacrifices to the new secular god, Technology.[5]

The poet Anne Sexton presents a harsh vision of a modern hospital. She compares it to a factory where "bodies crucified" are shipped to be processed by machinery. She concludes that the procedures to prolong life jeopardize human dignity and threaten the survival of all human attributes. She concedes that we may be kept alive biologically, but accuses that patients are stripped of all evidence of their personhood.[6]

Both physicians and patients alike are victims of a process they seem unable to stop. There is a kind of technological imperative that seems to insist that if we invent a machine we are under obligation to use it. What we can do automatically becomes what we must do. Add to this pressure the doctor's legitimate fear of malpractice suits, which hang like a dark cloud over the whole medical profession, making physicians fearful of omitting any procedure that someone might later argue could have been beneficial. And so, when faced with a decision to treat or not to treat, no matter how terminally ill the patient may be, every effort will likely be made to prolong the dying. The net result is that what started out to be treatment ends up as torture.

The Reverend Robert Fraser, a pastor in Rockville, Maryland, satirizes the situation in the following paraphrase:

> *Medical science is my shepherd;*
> *I shall not want.*
> *It maketh me to lie down in hospital beds;*
> *It leadeth me beside the marvels of technology.*
> *It restoreth my brain waves;*
> *It maintains me in a persistent vegetative state for its*
> *   name's sake;*
> *The respirator and heart machine, they sustain me.*
> *Surely, coma and unconsciousness shall follow me all*
> *   the days of my continued breathing, and I will dwell in*
> *   the intensive care unit forever.*[7]

Neither the doctor nor patient wants this. There comes a point beyond which life extension is pointless; it becomes in reality death extension. Clearly, the quality of life should be a determining factor in the length of life, and the patient should have the right to decide what quality is acceptable.

What, then, can we do to ensure respect for patients' rights as death nears? Both the medical profession and the church are speaking out with increasing clarity as new technology mandates moral guidelines. The American Medical Association is on record as declaring it ethically appropriate to withhold treatment from patients who suffer from an irreversible coma. Statements from both the Roman Catholic Church and Protestant denominations also support the patient's right to refuse treatment when it promises little more than a burdensome prolongation of the dying process.

To secure recognition of this right to die when circumstances make it desirable, the majority of states have passed laws recognizing the legality of living wills. These documents are filed with one's family, pastor, and physician to indicate what a person prefers regarding when and how one's life ends. It is understandable that doctors trained to keep patients alive sometimes find it difficult to honor these directives, which would expedite a patient's death, but since the landmark court decision in 1976 that allowed the removal of life-support systems from Karen Anne Quinlan, physicians face a wave of such directives at nearly every level of government. Such a document might read as follows:

I wish to live a full and long life, but not at all costs. If my death is near and cannot be avoided, and if I have lost the ability to interact with others and have no reasonable chance of regaining this ability, or if my suffering is intense and irreversible, I do not want to have my life prolonged. I would then ask not to be subjected to surgery or resuscitation. Nor would I then wish to have life support from intensive care services or other life-prolonging procedures. . . . I would wish, rather, to have care which gives comfort and support, which facilitates my interaction with others to the extent that is possible, and which brings peace.[8]

Increasingly, more attention is given to the patient's autonomy, and physicians are more willing to collaborate with the dying about what options are available. The paternalistic tradition of the medical profession is crumbling under the emerging concept of the patient as a consumer.

Of course it is impossible to anticipate how we will die. An advantage of trying to consider the range of contingencies in advance of death and putting in writing what we wish done is that we free friends and family members from having to make difficult decisions on our behalf. Ideally, I believe most people would prefer to die as my grandfather did. I remember his death as being relatively painless and with a clear mind. He was able to receive the comfort of spiritual companionship and to speak last words of affection to all his loved ones. Unfortunately, no one can be assured of such passing. In his recent best-selling book, *How We Die*, Dr. Sherman Nuland describes the different ways in which human beings expire. Dying is sometimes harsh and even violent. This book is more than just a clinical accounting of what happens to the body; it goes a long way toward demystifying death.

As a pastor, I am disturbed by a phrase that I hear used with increasing frequency by both caregivers and lay people who talk about dying: "a good death." Generally this refers to the person who dies with equanimity, without fear, and full of faith. However, the very idea of a good death may impose an unnecessary burden upon the dying individual, implying that even in dying there is a right way and a wrong way to do it! Americans are so performance oriented that even here we may be guilty of placing a cruel expectation both upon those we love and ourselves by using this phrase. Only when a person experiences death according to his or her own wishes can we say that a good death has occurred.

Happily, we have new resources available in most communities to alleviate some of the trauma. I am thinking especially of hospice care, which makes it easier for people who are dying to stay at home and be in the company of those who understand that love and tenderness may in the last analysis mean far more to the one who is terminally ill than a heavy dose of narcotics. As a clergyman, I am also aware of how blessed a dying patient is if at an earlier age he or she has committed to memory some of the great consolation passages of Scripture, such as the Twenty-third Psalm, or the lyrics of some of the faith-affirming hymns of the church. Hearing these familiar words and joining in the repeating of them can be a source of courage and enormous strength.

The fear of intense suffering or extended senility has led many elderly people to be more proactive in determining when they die. The overwhelming response to the recent book *Final Exit*, which became an overnight best-seller, revealed a groundswell of concern surfacing in our nation about when and how we die. Nothing stated here should be interpreted as advocacy for assisted suicide, but I believe we have come to a time in history when hastening death is an option that must be considered more seriously. The title "death doctor" has threatening connotations, but anyone close to the medical profession knows that most doctors from time to time have hastened a patient's death. Nearly always this is done as an act of mercy and is implemented either by offering excessive painkillers or by simply withholding treatment. What we are talking about here may be seen by some people as passive euthanasia, a widespread practice even now.

Ethical problems become considerably more acute when we move to active euthanasia. Christians are deeply committed to the sacredness of human life, yet we have already noted that the old understanding of a natural death no longer exists because of all the life-extending technology now available. The only country in the world where active euthanasia has the support of the law is the Netherlands, where some five thousand persons each year die this way.

Legislation to permit the practice in the United States has come close to passage in several states and in 1994 was passed in Oregon, though its constitutionality most likely will be challenged in the courts. Those who support this option must answer the counterarguments about starting down the slippery slope toward making it too easy to take the lives of people who should continue living. There are legitimate anxieties about death decisions occurring without adequate legal safeguards, and it would be tragic in a country where medical care is so expensive if older citizens ever felt pressured to request premature death in order to avoid becoming a financial burden to their families. The Hemlock Society, which supports the right of active euthanasia, is a growing movement in our country and portends a heated debate on our immediate national horizon. The inability thus far of the state of Michigan to convict Dr. Jack Kevorkian of murder for the part he played in multiple assisted suicides is a sign of how public opinion is changing and of what the future may hold.

The decisions we make about when and how to die are uniquely personal, and no one should feel pressured to act on any alternative. Some people may approach life's end as advised in the famous poem by Dylan Thomas and "rage, rage, against the dying of the light," while others may reject his advice and prefer to "go gentle into that good night."[9] In Luke's account of the elderly Simeon, who waited in the temple to see the promised Messiah, you may recall that when his long vigil was over and his hope was finally fulfilled that he prayed, "Lord, now lettest thou thy servant depart in peace . . ." (Luke 2:29). What an appropriate prayer as we approach death! And one more likely to be answered if we have given prior thought to how we want to exit the world. Christians can die with the confidence of the apostle Paul, who said, "We know that when this tent we live in—our body here on earth—is torn down, God will have a house in heaven for us to live in, a home he himself has made, which will last forever" (2 Corinthians 5:1, GNB).

It is reported that on a dark day in a New England town, residents became acutely upset because the sky looked so threatening and ominous. Ralph Waldo Emerson was walking down the street when a hysterical woman ran up to him, shouting, "Oh, Mr. Emerson, the world is coming to an end! What are we going to do?" With utmost calm, the wise old gentleman replied, "Never mind, my dear, we can get along quite well without it."

Chapter 9

Celebrating Your Deathday

The woman who summoned me to her bedside knew she was dying and wanted to discuss with her pastor the plans for her funeral. She said, "The next celebration in my life will be my deathday."

We are accustomed to celebrating birthdays, but it sounds strange to talk about a deathday celebration. We celebrate our arrival, so why not celebrate our departure? There is, in fact, one place in the United States where funerals have traditionally had a decidedly celebrative tone. The burials of black people in New Orleans are famous for their jazz musicians who accompany the procession as the body of the deceased is transported toward the grave.

But, for most of us, this seems almost anachronistic. How would you feel if some of the customs associated with our coming were transferred to mark our going? Suppose we knew the exact date of when we would die and used some of the same ways we remember our birthday to anticipate our deathday. At middle age we could begin counting our years from the other end, calculating how many we have left rather than how many we have behind us!

Suppose, for example, you knew that on June 10, 2003, you were going to die. How do you think you would feel each year when this date rolled around? Imagine having your friends gather for a surprise deathday party and singing "Happy Deathday to You." Instead of the candles on the cake representing the accumulation of years, suppose the cake would have a diminishing number of candles each year to indicate how many years were ahead. People who are very old often take great pleasure in asking others to guess how old they are, but I doubt if there would be much pleasure in boasting how few years they have left. Though we enjoy celebrating the anniversary of our entrance into the world, we probably would feel considerably ambivalent about celebrating the anniversary of our expected exit.

Scripture indicates that the apostle Paul would have considered a deathday celebration quite appropriate, for he said repeatedly that he looked forward to death with joyful anticipation. If given the choice between staying in the world or leaving it, Paul said he would be hard-pressed to choose—not because he wasn't ready to go but because he felt responsible about completing his obligations in this life before dying. He felt sure that being with Christ in the next life would be far better than anything experienced here. Dying was a transition he anticipated with no sadness. Like the elderly woman who summoned me to her bedside to plan her funeral, Paul shared her judgment that the arrival of one's deathday should be cause for celebration.

Such positive thoughts about dying are generally alien to us. We can more readily identify with the old man who stood on the street corner and begged from every young passerby, "How about helping an old fellow out by giving me a little of your allotted time?" Few people look forward to death in our generation. We are at home here, and we prefer the comforts of our known dwelling to the uncertainty of what lies before us.

When we are young or in the prime of life, it is understandable that death seems threatening, for, like Paul, we too have an agenda of responsibilities, hopes, and dreams that we would like to finish before we die. At these earlier stages of life it is easier to identify with the young Jesus, who also recoiled from the threat of death that night in the garden of Gethsemane. The Gospels report that Jesus was greatly distressed and troubled at the prospect of dying. "If it be possible, let this cup pass from me" (Matthew 26:37-40), he prayed. Because of similar reactions to the danger of early death, we too regard it as an enemy to be avoided at all costs. We lay wagers with insurance companies about how long we can keep our enemy at bay, and when critical illness requires hospitalization, teams of people do everything in their power to keep us from surrendering.

We generally do not interpret walking "through the valley of the shadow of death" as being descriptive of all of life but only of life's final hours. However, there is a sense in which our entire life span is a walk through the "valley of death," beginning at our birth. We are always old enough to die, and we are always tilting forward toward our inevitable demise, which casts an ominous shadow over everything preceding it. Throughout life's journey, our enemy is always lurking nearby and may catch us by surprise or claim us before we are ready to go. Life is far more fragile than we usually admit to ourselves.

Our desire to prolong life and our anxiety about leaving this world would have made little sense to Paul and the members of the early church. Their attitude toward their approaching deathday indicates a view of human destiny in a much larger context. They regarded death not as an infringement on life but as life's fulfillment. In our own time, Pastor Dietrich Bonhoeffer manifested a similar attitude when he was brought from his prison cell to be executed by the Nazis. With a calm countenance, he said to his guards, "For you it is the end, but for me, a beginning." Bonhoeffer's comment echoes Paul's often-quoted statement, "For to me to live is Christ, and to die is gain" (Philippians 1:21). These men were not weighted down with sadness at the prospect of dying; they looked forward to the transition. Indeed, a deathday celebration may have made more sense to Paul than celebrating a birthday!

As has been noted, our society today is much more open in discussing death than at an earlier time, and older people are taking the initiative in planning their own funerals and making all the necessary directives and legal decisions well in advance of their dying. Even so, one strange thing that has caught my ear is the reticence of older adults to say forthrightly, "When I *die* . . ." A more common euphemism prevails: "If *anything* happens to me . . ." Perhaps this is just a way to soften the awkwardness of broaching the subject of death with those whom we love.

Another thing I have noticed is the way some older adults

are able to make jokes about death. I consider a sense of humor an asset in nearly every situation, and here too, this seems to be the case. For example, when playwright George Abbott went to see his doctor at age ninety-six to get a pacemaker, his physician told him it would wear down in a decade and that he would then have to have it replaced. Abbott complained, "You mean I'm going to have to come back here in ten years and go through all this again?" And in answer to the question, "How are you getting along?" Robert Benchley replied, "Fine, except for an occasional heart attack."

A woman of advanced age stopped me at our senior center to tell me a "funny story," one she considered appropriate to share with a clergyman. She said a pastor was visiting an old lady and asked her if she ever thought about the hereafter. "Oh yes, every day," she replied. "When I walk from one room to another looking for things, I am always asking myself, 'What am I here after?'" While such humor may fall short of celebrating death, it surely indicates an ability to contemplate its coming. (Perhaps laughter is a way we release the tension we feel when we consider our approaching death.)

No longer is the dominant note of funerals a mournful dirge. We are making significant changes in the way we conduct them. Because of relatives and friends who are left behind, there will of course always be some sadness felt as people accept painful separations, but expressions of grief must never be the last word at the funeral of a Christian.

One symptomatic change becoming more common is the use of a new vocabulary. Increasingly, the heading on the order of worship reads, "A Celebration of the Life of . . .," naming the deceased. This suggests that the people gathered are there to remember the one who has died and presumably to offer praise to God as they recall his or her life.

Sometimes, however, the service does not rise much beyond the level of remembering. On occasion it almost seems that those present are worshiping the dead. And, not surprisingly, people who are not close to the church tend to secularize the service in ways that border on candid offensiveness or as if those attending were at a roast instead of a worship service. This trend was noted recently in a column by "Miss Manners," who complained about the hypocrisy of much that is said at funerals in order to avoid hurting the feelings of living relatives and to protect the dead from embarrassment. She sees the dilemma of putting forth as good a case as possible for the deceased while keeping it plausible for the mourners.[1] This dilemma can be resolved if God is the focus of attention rather than the one who is dead.

If a service is not centered in God, it ceases to be a service of worship. Reflections about the deceased are appropriate only if the celebration credits the Creator with praise for all evidence of goodness and blessing. The celebrative tone is further fostered by faith-affirming hymns and biblical proclamations that offer the people assembled an opportunity to glorify God. In my own congregation, there are times when the funeral even incorporates a celebrative liturgical dance.

Several current practices compromise the possibility of the funeral service's being understood as a celebration. It is commonplace, for example, to refer to the event as a memorial service, terminology that suggests looking backward rather than forward. Grounds for celebration are shaky indeed if the backward look is the major emphasis, for a Christian funeral anticipates God's tomorrow and an ultimate consummation of all we have known and done here.

Scheduling funerals in mortuary chapels instead of in churches is another practice that deprives family and friends of sacred associations. This alternative may be an appropriate choice for people who have lived outside the faith community, but it imposes an unnecessary hardship for believers. It is much easier to worship in a familiar setting where we are accustomed to hearing the central tenets of the Christian faith proclaimed. No doubt the popularity of the funeral-home chapel can be accounted for by morticians who urge their use for their own convenience, but it is time for pastors and church leaders to protest this practice and insist that funerals of the faithful be celebrated in the sanctuary of the deceased's congregation.

Many older people today have an attitude toward death that is not found in Scripture. They begin to see death as a friend, whereas the Bible consistently refers to it as an enemy. When I was a child, death seemed so far away that I did not feel threatened by it, but I thought that the older I became the more afraid of death I would be. I imagined it would be terrible to grow old and know that death was near. But now that I am almost seventy, I find just the opposite to be true. Death seems less and less threatening. I now understand how after a long life it is not only possible but probable that death can be embraced as a blessing. Yet the Bible never depicts death as something to be welcomed. Both the Old Testament and the New Testament consistently view death as an enemy, never as a friend. The Psalmist writes:

For the enemy pursued me:
  he has crushed my life to the ground;
  he has made me sit in darkness with those long dead.
            —Psalm 143:3, Goodspeed

Paul the apostle refers to death as "the last enemy" and the Book of Revelation looks forward to the end of time when the enemy, death, "shall be no more" (1 Corinthians 15:26; Revelation 21:4).

How can we reconcile this biblical imagery with the more welcoming attitude toward death expressed by many older people, especially those who suffer failing health? First, we must recognize that longevity was the exception in earlier eras, and, as we have already seen, when younger people die, death does seem like an intrusive enemy. Second, we must examine our Christian faith. The primary Good News of the gospel is that Christ conquered death. So, we Christians believe we are now beyond the permanent reach of our ancient foe. This conviction is our justification for celebrating at funerals. Christian funerals are best understood as victory celebrations. Our enemy has suffered a major defeat. We rejoice because the power of death is no match for the power of God. Furthermore, Scripture promises that as Jesus was raised from the dead, so will we too be lifted up into newness of life. Thus, every Sunday is a repetitive celebration of the Resurrection, which occurred on the first day of the week. The apostle Paul speaks for all believers when he exclaims, "Death is swallowed up in victory. O death, where is thy sting?" (1 Corinthians 15:54-55).

It is easier to celebrate deathdays if we have some understanding of what lies beyond death. The unknown always creates anxiety, which is surely the reason many people are reluctant to give up what they know in exchange for a mystery. Unlike those who lived in the Middle Ages, we modern people tend to think of this world as God's main staging area, and of the afterlife, at best, as an epilogue. But we are beginning to see evidence that we may have had a very provincial view of the universe. We realize that our heavy emphasis on materialism has failed to take into account those spiritual dimensions of reality not detected by scientific procedures. Indeed, there is a growing consensus that our religious word "spirit" may coincide more closely with the nature of ultimate reality than the secular word "energy." People today seem more open to the belief that there is far more "out there" than we can see or touch or measure.

Except for those reared in the traditions of western Europe, most of the world seldom questions the primacy of spiritual reality. Could it be that our blindness to the spiritual is a main cause of the many modern maladies we suffer?

We can gain a better understanding of the other side of dying if we grasp the distinction between time and eternity. Popular thought perpetuates a misperception of eternity as simply an extension of time. A perfect illustration of this is "Amazing Grace," one of the best-loved hymns of Christendom. Consider its linear imagery:

> *When we've been there ten thousand years,*
> *Bright shining as the sun,*
> *We've no less days to sing God's praise*
> *Than when we've first begun.*

Eternal life is more accurately understood not as a prolongation of life but as quality life, not as life subject to temporal conditions but as life beyond all sense of past and future.

Theologian Paul Tillich published a helpful volume of

sermons some years ago titled *The Eternal Now*. His theme drives home the point that no matter how far time is extended, it does not become eternity. By definition, time is duration, whereas eternity is present, permanent reality. There is no such thing as time after time has ended, but there is eternity above time and encompassing time. Or, to put it another way, eternal life cannot be arrived at by adding days to days; it is best described as unlimited life all at once!

Something Mozart once said about a musical composition illustrates the concept:

> *When my soul gets heated, and if nothing disturbs me, the piece grows longer and brighter until, however long it is, it is all finished at once in my mind, so that I can see it at a glance as if it were a pretty picture or a pleasing person. Then I don't hear the notes one after another, as they are hereafter to be played, but it is as if in my fancy they were all at once.*

Since we live within time, it is not surprising that this concept is difficult to grasp or that we should sing, "When we've been there ten thousand years," but our failure to draw this distinction between time and eternity has left us with an erroneous impression.

The Christian hope is not for a continuation of life but for eternal communion with God, who transcends time. The Gospel of John supports this distinction where we read, "This *is* eternal life, that they may know You, the only true God . . ." (John 17:3, NKJV). The author is not speaking quantitatively but qualitatively. The promise of eternal life is for life at a new level. It is much more than mere survival. It means living in a dimension of spiritual reality where time-keeping devices would serve no purpose.

Happily, however, we can experience wisps of this spiritual reality within the confines of time. Again, the Gospel of John reflects this understanding where we read, "he who hears My word and believes in Him who sent Me *has* everlasting life, and shall not come into judgment, but *has passed* from death into life" (John 5:24, NKJV)—present tense, not future! We can have a foretaste today of what we will enjoy in all its fullness tomorrow. We celebrate the certainty of finding on the other side of dying those precious spiritual realities partially experienced on this side, such as love, joy, beauty, and peace.

The crude cosmology of Scripture sometimes turns people off with its description of heaven and hell and its implication that heaven is "up there" and hell "down below." We should not be misled by such language. Obviously, we do not live in a triple-decker universe. Such imagery is best understood as symbolic speech. It is probably more accurate to think of heaven and hell as coming to us rather than our going to them. When something exuberant happens to us, we exclaim, "This is heaven!" And when we suffer some horrible event, we mourn, "I've been through hell." These are spiritual states and not places on a cosmic map.

Simply put, to be in heaven is to be in the presence of God, and to be in hell is to be cut off from God. Clearly, this is not literal speech but poetic speech. It is the Bible's way of attempting to describe the indescribable. To picture heaven as a place where the streets are paved with gold is not very complimentary to our human sense of values. There is little to be gained by trying to describe the furniture of heaven or to gauge the temperature of hell.

Comparing this life with the life beyond demands a larger vocabulary than we have words to express. Inevitably we are left with a broad latitude of mystery, but one thing we can affirm with confidence is that the God who meets us on this side of dying is the same God who meets us on the other side. Just as goodness and mercy have followed us all the days of our lives, so shall we "dwell in the house of the Lord forever" (Psalm 23:6). Jesus' statement, "In my Father's house are many rooms" (John 14:2, NIV) tells us that this world is only one of God's rooms and that at death we move into another.

Not all our questions will be answered before our deathday comes, but this much is clear: life and death are bound up together. Those first Christians endured beyond anyone else in the ancient world because they were convinced that their lives transcended their short time on earth. They believed they had already sampled the spiritual reality of the hereafter through their communion with God in the here and now.

In her recent autobiography, *Ordinary Time*, Nancy Mairs writes about the place of faith in the cycles of her life, and in the final chapter she tells about how she and her husband are facing his encounter with death. She concludes that though death's presence is unwelcome, yet "far from rendering us morose, it has made us spiritually alert and vigorous." She adds, "The extraordinary benefit of death . . . lies in its redemptive quality. Horribly constrained in a body that can no longer roll over in bed reliably . . . I have never felt freer to cherish and celebrate . . ."[2]

Celebration is appropriate to all of life, including death, for as the apostle Paul said:

> *Whether we live, we live unto the Lord; and whether we die, we die unto the Lord: whether we live therefore, or die, we are the Lord's (Romans 14:8).*

In the catacombs of Rome where the underground church buried its dead, many of the tombs are not inscribed with birth dates, only death dates. This practice reflects the early Christian belief that deathdays are more important than birthdays. A major difference is that when we die we enter a far better life than the life that began on our birthday. The world of the spirit to which we go is far more to be desired than the world we leave behind.

Notes

Introduction

1. Robert Browning, "Rabbi ben Ezra," in *Robert Browning's Poetry*, ed. James F. Loucks (New York: W. W. Norton and Co., 1979).

Chapter 1

1. W. B. Yeats, "Sailing to Byzantium," in *The Poems of W. B. Yeats: A New Edition*, ed. Richard Finneran (New York: Macmillan, 1928).
2. T. S. Eliot, "The Love Song of J. Alfred Prufrock," in *Collected Poems 1909-1962* (New York: Harcourt Brace & Company, 1963). Used by permission.
3. St. Augustine, Sermon 108 in *Select Library of Nicene and Post-Nicene Fathers of the Christian Church*, ed. Phillip Schaff (Grand Rapids: Wm. B. Eerdmans Publishing Co., 1956), 440, quoted in Eugene C. Bianchi, *Aging as a Spiritual Journey* (New York: The Crossroad Publishing Company, 1992), 132.
4. Linda George, lecture at Southeastern Gerontological Society, Charlotte, North Carolina, April 21, 1994.
5. Ibid.
6. Sharon Curtin, *Nobody Ever Died of Old Age* (Waltham, Mass.: Atlantic Monthly Press, 1972), 193-194.
7. Anna Mae Halgrim Seaver, "My World Now: Life in a Nursing Home, from the Inside," *Newsweek*, June 27, 1994, 11.
8. Daniel Goleman, "Mental Decline in Aging Need Not Be Inevitable," *New York Times*, April 26, 1994, B5.
9. Robert Burns, "To a Louse," stanza 8, lines 43-44.
10. Reuel Howe, *How to Stay Younger While Growing Older* (Waco: Word Books, 1974), 125.
11. William Lyon Phelps, as appeared in a church newsletter, n.d.

Chapter 2

1. Jitsuo Morikawa, American Baptist News Service, Division of Communications, September 1974.

Chapter 3

1. William Shakespeare, *Henry IV*, part II, act 5, scene 5.
2. Alexander Pope, *Essay on Man*, Epistle II, line 247.
3. See Luke 2:27.
4. See Titus 2:2-3.
5. See John 21:18.
6. National Interfaith Coalition on Aging (1975), quoted in *Generations*, Winter 1991, 62.
7. William Shakespeare, *Macbeth*, Act 5, Scene 5, line 11.
8. Armistead Maupin, *Tales of the City* (New York: Harper and Row, 1978).
9. André Gide, *Journals* (1951), quoted in *Generations*, Winter 1991, 61.
10. *Green Winter* by Elise Maclay, published in 1989 by and soon to be reissued in paperback (1995) by Henry Holt and Company, New York, N.Y. Used by permission of author.
11. Thomas Hood, "I Remember, I Remember," stanza 4.
12. Princeton Religious Research Center, as reported in *The Christian Century*, June 29-July 6, 1994, 636.
13. Simone Weil, as quoted by Father Leo Smith in *Spirituality and Recovery* (Pompano Beach: Health Communications, Inc., 1985), 53.
14. Elisabeth Lukas, lecture at Victor Frankl Institute of Logotherapy, Berkeley, California, July 1984, quoted in William Gould, *Vicktor E. Frankl: Life with Meaning* (Belmont, Calif.: Brooks/Cole Publishing Co., 1993), 150.

Chapter 4

1. Søren Kierkegaard, *Purity of Heart Is to Will One Thing* (New York: Harper and Brothers, 1938).
2. Alexander Pope, *Thoughts on Various Subjects*.
3. Silvia Bigio, "A Simple Man," *Ulisse 2000*, July 1994, 132.
4. *Green Winter* by Elise Maclay, published in 1989 by and soon to be reissued in paperback (1995) by Henry Holt and Company, New York, N.Y. Used by permission of author.
5. "A Mighty Fortress Is Our God" (*Ein Feste Burg*), written by Martin Luther, trans. Frederich Henry Hedge.
6. Information Office, The Peace Corps, Washington, D.C.
7. Allan Luks, Peggy Payne, *The Healing Power of Doing Good: The Health and Spiritual Benefits of Helping Others* (New York: Fawcett Columbine, 1991).
8. Ibid.

9. Pitirim Sorokin, *Altruistic Love, A Study of American "Good Neighbors" and Christian Saints* (Boston: Beacon Press, 1950), 197-199.

Chapter 5

1. Paul Tournier, *Learn to Grow Old* (New York: Harper and Row, 1972), 195.
2. Research project at the University of Georgia by Dr. Leonard Poom, gerontologist.

Chapter 6

1. T. J. Moore,"The Cholesterol Myth," *Atlantic* Magazine, September 1989.
2. Jane E. Brody, "Hearts May Safely Flutter over Valentine Chocolates," *New York Times*, February 14, 1994.
3. Barbara Silverstone, Helen Kandel Hyman, *Growing Older Together: A Couple's Guide to Understanding and Coping with the Challenges of Later Life* (New York: Pantheon, 1992), 7.
4. Statistics from Alliance for Aging Research, University of California at Los Angeles.
5. John Milton, *Paradise Lost*, quoted in Norman Cousins, *Anatomy of an Illness As Perceived by the Patient: Reflections on Healing and Regeneration* (New York: Bantam Books, 1979), 67.
6. Norman Cousins, *Anatomy of an Illness* (New York: Bantam Books, 1979).
7. Ibid, 66.
8. Deepak Chopra, *Ageless Body, Timeless Mind: The Quantum Alternative to Growing Old* (New York: Harmony Books, 1993).

Chapter 7

1. Robert Seymour, *Whites Only* (Valley Forge: Judson Press, 1991).
2. Sarah Louise Delany, Annie Elizabeth Delany, with Amy Hill Hearth, *Having Our Say: The Delany Sisters' First Hundred Years* (New York: Kodansha America, 1993).
3. *Green Winter* by Elise Maclay, published in 1989 by and soon to be reissued in paperback (1995) by Henry Holt and Company, New York, N.Y. Used by permission of author.
4. William Shakespeare, *Macbeth*, Act 5, Scene 3, line 22.
5. Paul Tillich, *Love, Power, and Justice* (London: Oxford University Press, 1954), 25-26.
6. William Mountford, *Euthanasy or Happy Talk Towards the*

End of Life (Cambridge: Metcalf and Co., 1848), 3-4, quoted in Eugene Bianchi, *Aging as a Spiritual Journey* (New York: The Crossroads Publishing Company, 1992), 183.

7. Archibald MacLeish, "With Age Wisdom" in *Collected Poems 1917–1982* (Boston: Houghton Mifflin Co., 1985), 422.

8. Dag Hammarskjöld, *Markings* (New York: Alfred A. Knopf, 1964), 56.

9. Robert Browning, "Rabbi ben Ezra," in *Robert Browning's Poetry*, ed. James F. Loucks (New York: W. W. Norton and Co., 1979).

Chapter 8

1. Paul Bowles, *The Sheltering Sky* (London: Flamingo, 1993), 212.

2. Leo Tolstoy, "The Death of Ivan Ilyich," trans. Lynn Solotaroff (New York: Bantam Books, 1981).

3. Jacob K. Javits, "Life, Death and Human Dignity," *New York Times*, August 18, 1985.

4. Daniel Callahan, The Hastings Center, Institute of Society, Ethics, and Life Science. As quoted in a sermon by the Reverend Michael Scoggins, First Baptist Church, Springfield, Mass., May 27, 1984.

5. Richard Lamm, lectures at Pacific School of Religion, January 14, 1985.

6. Anne Sexton, "August 17th" *Words for Dr. Y*, (New York: Houghton Mifflin, 1976), 73.

7. Robert Fraser of Rockville, Maryland, quoted in Lecture III at the Pacific School of Religion by Richard Lamm, January 1985.

8. Sissela Bok for *The New England Journal of Medicine*, August 12, 1976.

9. Dylan Thomas, "Do Not Go Gentle into That Good Night," in *Poems of Dylan Thomas* (New York: New Directions Publishing Co., 1957).

Chapter 9

1. Judith Martin, "A Lament for Old-Fashioned Funerals," *The News and Observer*, Raleigh, North Carolina. March 27, 1994.

2. Nancy Mairs, *Ordinary Time: Cycles in Marriage, Faith, and Renewal* (Boston: Beacon Press, 1993), quoted in *The Christian Century*, March 23-30, 1994, 227.